# FROM SAIL TO STEAM

## Gerard, Back at Sea

by J. R. Hathaway

Illustrated by M. C. Arroyo

DORRANCE PUBLISHING CO
EST. 1920
PITTSBURGH, PENNSYLVANIA 15238

Dorrance Publishing Co
585 Alpha Drive
Pittsburgh, PA 15238
Visit our website at *www.dorrancebookstore.com*

ISBN: 979-8-88527-297-1
eISBN: 979-8-88527-432-6

# DEDICATION

To all future authors, young and old. If you have a story to tell, write it down and share it. You never know how many lives you will touch.

# Introduction

Gerard Koper (1868-1942) was my maternal grandfather. He was born in Den Helder, Holland, which is a small naval city on the North Sea. He came from a long line of sailors. At age eleven he went to sea with his father, Captain Hendrikus Antonius Koper, aboard the *Polux*.

Grandpa Koper died before I was born in 1943. So, I never knew him. Before passing away, he wrote letters to my mother, Viola Koper Romer, providing detailed stories about his career as a sailor. My mother, along with my sister, Janice Caroline Romer Sherman, recorded those letters in a paper they entitled "From Sail to Steam". While growing up, I often heard the family talk about grandpa's rich Dutch history and sailing career. It sounded so romantic and exciting and I became interested in learning more about his life and my own Dutch heritage.

My initial research and travels to Holland and Belgium in 1981 and 2013 provided information for my first book, *From Windmills to Waves, Gerard, Little Dutch Sailor*, published in 2016. That work included stories of Gerard's childhood in Holland and his adventuresome first year of sailing on a large, four-masted sailing ship.

In subsequent years I was able to conduct additional research in order to present this work, *From Sail to Steam, Gerard, Back at Sea*, which follows Gerard's life forward until his death.

It must be said that grandpa's initial reporting to my mother included his best memories of the many seas and ports that he visited. Wherever possible in this work I have provided the modern and updated spellings to provide a more complete and accurate accounting of his sailing career.

In spite of this, I feel that grandpa's rich and exciting life is worth documenting and preserving for my own children and grandchildren, as well as for others who can only dream of adventure. I am proud of the rich heritage that he left.

# Contents

# CHAPTER 1
# The Blood of a Sailor

It was a glorious, clear summer day when the *Polux* glided into the port of Nieuwediep in Den Helder, Holland, where they were met by town's folk with a warm hometown welcome. The people were waving their arms and little Dutch flags as the children jumped up and down with excitement at seeing this majestic sight. They strained their eyes and tried to spot their fathers standing proudly up on the top decks.

Captain Koper handed each his share of profits and said, "Thank you, gentlemen, for getting us through it all. It was a long year and a difficult voyage. You are now home and may go to your families if you'd like."

Some of the men wanted to keep on working, while others returned home. The ship was towed into dry dock to have the barnacles scraped off the bottom and the ship repainted inside and out. Sails had to be repaired and the running gear overhauled. The yards and mast needed varnishing.

Gerard and his father, the captain, then turned away from the ship and hiked along the dikes toward their home and little farm.

"Papa, a sailor's life is really hard work, isn't it?" Gerard quickly spoke up.

"That's true, Gerard," the captain nodded his head as he replied. He raised an eyebrow as he was somewhat surprised at his son's admission.

As they walked, Gerard dared to continue. "I had always dreamed of traveling the world in a big sailing vessel like you do. It sounded so exciting. But, it's not just fun and exciting travel with new places to explore. I thought that my crewmates would naturally be my buddies. But they were all so much older than I and so experienced. At first, I knew that they didn't like me and didn't trust me to pull my weight. They could see that I was young and small for my age of eleven. Also, being your son didn't help me to win their respect. They were afraid that I would reveal their secrets."

The captain gave a little chuckle of understanding. "I believe that was the case, Gerard."

Gerard continued, "I think that my reputation started to improve after we all survived rounding the Horn (Cape Horn) in a terrible storm. The waves were crashing over the decks, throwing our helpless ship from side to side and up and down, threatening to send us into the jagged rocks of the coast. I'll admit that I was really scared, but I tried to hide it. The truth is I felt like crying. We were soaked to the bone and shivering from the cold. The only comfort was hard tack (very hard unleavened bread) and coffee. That was the first time that I could admit to myself that I had made a big mistake by running away in the early morning hours to stow away aboard the *Polux*. I realized that I should never have left our cozy Dutch cottage in Den Helder."

As they progressed along the dikes, Gerard continued, "When you used to be gone for a year or more on a big sailing, I would dream of the far-off, exotic lands you visited. My teacher gave me books so I could follow your routes from sea to sea and country to country. I could only imagine going to Africa, China, the Philippines, or South America. I thought the sailing vessel would just glide gracefully through the seas. I wished that I could go with you. However, those thoughts were just childhood dreams.

In reality, the life of a sailor was really hard and dangerous work. In the year aboard the *Polux* I was forced to face many grown-up experiences. I had to do lots of unpleasant jobs aboard the ship, like cleaning the mess (kitchen), mopping the decks, and peeling lots and lots of potatoes. There seemed to be no end to the piles of potatoes. I hated the hard tack and boring diet. I had never had coffee before, but I learned to appreciate it as that was the main beverage of sailors. I craved the fresh food from our farm and occasional sweet treats that Mama gave me at home."

"I also missed home, Gerard," Papa admitted.

Gerard continued. "Papa, I know that I was lucky to even survive the sailing. It would have been easy to get swept overboard in high seas. Luckily, we didn't lose one sailor. I could have gotten yellow fever or malaria or typhoid fever (all potentially fatal diseases) or died from an injury aboard the ship. I now know and understand how dangerous your work is. Papa, you are responsible for getting your ship and crew successfully around the world and back again, all the while trading spices, cheese, and small goods from country to country.

I understand that you did it to earn money for the Koper family as well as the shipping company. It was not fun for you. It was a big responsibility. Many people were counting on you. You have gained the respect of so many people we visited, from South America, China, Indonesia, and South Africa. It was obvious to me that they now consider you a trusted friend. You have won their admiration. Although I'll always miss you when you are away for so long, I will now be able to imagine where you are and what you are doing."

In a rare moment of intimacy, Gerard paused and softly said, "I love you, Papa." Those words did not come easily to a child in Holland. Gerard didn't know what would follow.

With a sideways grin and a gentle hug, Papa willingly confessed, "Gerard, when I found you hiding away in a storage bin aboard the *Polux*, I was furious. I was just embarking on an important worldwide voyage. I had so much on my mind. I was facing a difficult sailing, with valuable cargo to distribute to many ports. I was responsible for a large crew that had to learn to work together. Many people were counting on me. My job and reputation were at stake. The last thing I needed was a child, especially one who was as small and inexperienced as you. It would be just one more worry and a big responsibility. I knew that your mama would expect me to deliver you back home in one piece. But, in time you certainly surprised me and become a worthy young sailor. I am proud of you, Gerard."

That was the first time Papa had ever expressed such pride and appreciation of his son. Compliments were hard to come by in Dutch families, especially for this stern captain.

Gerard was hardly recognizable from a year and a half ago, when the skinny little kid slipped aboard the full-rigged sailing vessel and stowed away on the *Polux*. He moved from storage bin to storage bin, avoiding crew members until he was discovered by his own papa, the captain. By that time, the ship was well underway and there was no turning back to deliver Gerard back to Den Helder. Both Gerard and Captain Koper were stuck with each other. Gerard was now a member of the crew. He set out to prove himself worthy of the job.

After a few difficult months and in spite of his age and size, he had carried out the duties of a new sailor aboard this huge vessel. As the lowest ranking member of the crew, he was always called upon for mundane tasks. In the process, Gerard grew stronger and became respected by his skeptical fellow crewmates and, it now seems, by his father, the captain. He had carried his weight. In addition, Gerard had gained a new respect and admiration for his papa and the difficult responsibility of safely guiding the sailing ship around the world and back home again.

Those complex feelings revealed themselves as the pair, father and son, made their way from the docks to Mama and their own little farmhouse on the outskirts of Den Helder, Holland. The tulip bulbs had all been harvested and stored in the barn, and the garden vegetables were flourishing in the cool summer climate of North Holland. As school would be on break, Gerard would have to wait until fall to tell his friends all about the amazing ports of call that he had visited around the world.

He would tell of the festive, colorful South American city of Santiago, Chile, with a backdrop of high snow-capped mountains sloping into the bright blue Pacific Ocean. In the flat country of Holland, he had never experienced such a sight.

He found himself in the chaotic port of Hong Kong where he saw vessels of all types and sizes from all over the world and a culture far different from the familiar order of Holland. Papa had taken him for a ride in a rickshaw which was powered by a small man with shafts across his shoulders and running as fast as a horse. They had enjoyed a bowl of noodles as they watched crowds of Chinese noisily conduct business on the streets. Papa introduced Gerard to his clients as he engaged in trade. Gerard could see that his father had to be authoritative, but friendly, to accomplish good deals for the company.

Then the *Polux* had sailed on to the Sunda Strait. Gerard recalled experiencing the violence of a volcano, Krakatau. "Papa, the volcano was so scary. I had read about volcanos in school, but it was very different actually being in the middle of it all. The sky lit up bright red. The more experienced sailors knew what would follow. They shouted, 'Volcano' just as the ground began to rumble and shake. The power of the explosion was unbelievable. The island simply blew up into a million pieces and disappeared below the sea."

"We were all in shock and stood frozen in fear. The smells were awful. There were dead men, women, and children everywhere, floating among burning debris from ships. I hated pulling dead people, especially children my own age, out of the fiery sea. That's something I'll never forget. It was sickening. The island was completely destroyed. I wondered if anyone back home would hear about that."

In truth though, the voyage was not all work and no play. Gerard also had some fun times. In South Africa he rode horses and chased kangaroos in the svelte. He saw the largest diamond mines in the world at The Kimberly Mine, or The Big Hole, in Cape Town, South Africa. He learned to joke with the crew. They laughed at the sight of huge fish jumping up into their ship and providing a fresh meal or two. Gerard had grown up. He now held his head high and walked with an air of confidence.

"Mama, Mama, we're home!" Gerard broke his pensive mood as he shouted. He wildly waved his arms and called out to her at the first sight of their little Dutch cottage. He burst away from Papa and raced full speed ahead down the dike, past his uncles' cottages, Mama's small vegetable garden, and into her arms as she pushed through the door, wiping her hands on her little lace apron.

"You won't believe all the places we've been. I'm sorry I ran away from home and stowed away on Papa's ship. But I worked hard. Papa paid me money." He had so much to say and the words just tumbled out as he handed his mother the money that Papa had paid him.

By that time, Papa and Mama were in a tight embrace and full of their own messages. They had missed each other so much. Tears of relief streamed down Mama's cheeks. She could finally relax, knowing that Papa was back safely on dry land. In return, Papa had worried about Mama and the farm. But at first glance, the farm and home looked to be in good shape. Mama and the uncles had obviously worked hard to keep it all together while he was gone.

While sitting alone in her rocking chair for many long evenings, Mama's thoughts had often drifted to her husband and son, Gerard. She had received word from South America that Gerard was aboard with Papa. But that was not very comforting. It only increased her worries as she knew that Gerard had never before been out of their safe little town of Den Helder.

She also was aware of the many dangers they would face. She knew what a responsibility it was for Papa to steer the huge sailing vessel from port to port and to deal with the crew and port bosses along the way. She shivered at the thought of Gerard rounding the Horn, with its dangerous seas and rocky coast. She had heard news about the eruption of Krakatau and knew that the *Polux* could have been destroyed and the entire crew lost at sea. She worried how her young son would face such dangers and tragedy.

Those thoughts vanished immediately as they stood before her, safe and sound. She backed up a little and took a good, hard look with pride at her husband and son. After a few deep breaths, all settled down and entered the cottage to enjoy a good meal and tea.

Mama dearly loved her husband and son. There was no doubt in her mind that Gerard should now stay home and resume his chores around the farm and return to school in the fall. That was what she expected.

But that was not to be. For Papa was a sailor and sailors do not stay home for long. They live aboard ships, one after another. And now it was obvious that Gerard had also fallen in love with the sea.

However, Mama didn't realize that this calm would end so soon. In fact, Gerard only had a few weeks to gather his land legs before he felt the call of the sea once again. Papa's entire crew remained loyal to him and returned to the *Polux*, ready and willing to work. Papa took all of them, along with Gerard, to the shipping office and signed up for the next trip.

Demonstrating approval for Gerard's work of the previous year, Papa signed him up as 'light sailor', with a small raise from his previous position of 'boy'. This time, Gerard was not a stow-away. It was official. Gerard was proud to be one of the crew. Mama didn't like it, but she had no choice in the matter.

# CHAPTER 2
# Rio

Together once again, the crew of the *Polux* picked up her first cargo, Edam cheese, at the port of Nieuwediep, Holland. They were bound for Hamburg, Germany, and then to Rio de Janeiro in South America. In Hamburg they loaded heavy machinery, and then headed to Bremerhaven where they picked up two small locomotives. This was a big surprise for Gerard. He was accustomed to light loads of cheese, tea, spices and household goods. Now there was reason for concern about this heavy load as they headed out for their next voyage.

Dutch summers were short and fall was now approaching. Cold and rough seas were looming as they sailed out for the North Sea and the English Channel. They had the deck load on the 'well deck', located between the fore and main mast. It would take constant monitoring of the lashings to see that the locomotives stayed put and secure. Otherwise, they would get loose and wreck the ship.

With skillful sailing, they got off the English Channel with a strong breeze from the port quarter and settled course for the Azores Islands, southwest. Two days out of the channel the wind increased and turned into a gale in the Atlantic Ocean. They were compelled to shorten sail and hove-to (hold in same position) under reefed lower top sails and jib, and boy, did she blow! High seas crashed over the decks, which were constantly swamped. Everyone's thoughts were on the big load they were carrying. With every little lull in the storm some of the men went down the well deck from the poop deck to look and examine the two locomotives.

On the third day they tacked ship southwest, settled a little more sail and went on course to the Azores. They took up the slack on the lashings on the deck load and, luckily, everything was all right again. The only exception was the crew, who were soaked to the bone, tired, and hungry. Taking the bearings the next day at noon, they calculated that the gale had driven them off course about one hundred miles. The crew returned to their regular four-hour shifts and the cook served up warm meals again. The *Polux* proceeded on the way to the Azores.

As the weather improved, they passed the Azores and settled due south for the Brazilian coast. As they moved into the Gulf Stream and headed south it was getting warmer, which was a nice change for this Dutch crew. The wind shifted to north by east, so she came from the quarter and they settled the stun sails as well. As they sailed south, they neared steamship routes coming north from Rio. Steamships were a unique sight for the crew of this graceful sailing ship. One steamship captain reported that there was yellow fever (a serious illness spread by mosquitos) in Rio de Janeiro. This brought the captain and crew heightened concern about what lay ahead of them.

As the *Polux* sailed along, Gerard's duties were split between his usual watch duties, sewing sails and splicing ropes. At times, the captain and first mate took him in hand to the chart room, breaking him in on the finer points of navigation. This was an honor that Gerard did not take lightly. Nor did he brag about this to his mates. He had learned from his previous sailing that that might cause jealousy among the crew. As they were older and more experienced at sea, they would think that they, not Gerard, should be given the opportunity to learn a higher skill. He also knew that Papa had a part in giving him this privilege. He kept quiet about it, but did try to learn all that he could.

Sometimes they were all treated to a special meal of fried fish as flying fish leaped aboard. Porpoises, along with sharks, played around the ship. An occasional albatross flew by. All this helped to entertain the crew, as well as provide a variety to their boring diet.

Fun never lasted too long on a complex voyage such as this. When they were hailed by the pilot (a man who helps guide the ship into the harbor) at Rio de Janeiro, they were warned about the yellow fever there. As he advised, "You can probably make safe harbor here if you don't take any chances. The virus is pretty much under control here."

If it hadn't been for the heavy cargo of locomotives and heavy equipment aboard the *Polux*, they could have dropped anchor in Roads and discharged there. But they needed the help of big cranes to do the work. Two tugboats pulled them along the docks under the crane for unloading.

The port officials came aboard and ordered all hands to stay aboard and not to have any contact with the people on shore. That was sure tough luck for the boys who had sweethearts ashore. They'd have to miss them this trip. Gerard was too young to understand.

"The best cure for yellow fever is not to get it," ordered the captain to the disappointed crew.

The experienced old captain was wise to this part of the world and knew that yellow fever could wipe out his crew and halt their profitable voyage. He had anticipated this possibility before leaving Den Helder and laid in a good stock of rations. All their drinking water was boiled. Raw fruit had to be washed before eating. There was to be no contact with the natives. The only ones coming aboard were the stevedores, coming to unload, and they were examined every morning by a doctor before coming to work.

Due to these extra precautions, it took a week or more to unload the cargo and take on a new shipment for Southampton, England. Without losing a man, they got clearance and left harbor. They had escaped yellow fever for now. Then the *Polux* was off for the last leg of their voyage, a return to Nieuwediep.

With that short voyage over, Gerard and Papa had to face Mama once again. "Okay, Henry," Mama stood with her hands on her hips and a scowl on her face. "It's time for Gerard to catch up on his schooling. You cannot take him back to sea."

Papa and Gerard both knew that she was firm in her decision. They did not argue. Gerard listened attentively as Papa read his next orders aloud to Mama. Gerard was disappointed that he could not go this time. But he did understand. Seeing a pout come over Gerard's face, Mama emphatically ordered, "Gerard, you have been on two long sailings. You need to stay home for a while and catch up on your schooling."

Gerard's older brother was sent to sea with Papa while Gerard and his little brother, Anton, stayed behind.

Papa's new assignment was to captain the *Hildagonda*. Many of his crewmates from the *Polux* remained loyal to him and signed on to this new voyage. Their destination was Valparaiso in Argentina, around Cape Horn.

Gerard knew full well how dangerous the voyage would be as he recounted his own passage around the Horn.

Papa and Gerard's older brother left while life in Den Helder returned to normal.

Throughout the winter Gerard obediently returned to school and helped around the cottage and small farm in Den Helder. He had to help maintain the windmills, which were in constant motion. He knew that the windmills were vital to the economy of Holland. As Holland is a country below sea level, it is in constant danger of flooding. Too much seawater would ruin the tulips and vegetables. The water had to be pushed back to the canals and rivers, and back to the sea.

There was no school on Wednesday afternoons or Saturdays. As all Dutch children were expected to work and contribute to the household income, Gerard was put to work in a furniture shop where he learned about the furniture business and earned a little money. In the evenings he and Anton sawed wood and broke coke and turf to keep the home fires going. So, Gerard's life in Den Helder was typical for a Dutch child. But Gerard was always looking for a more exciting life, hopefully in sailing.

# CHAPTER 3
# The *Argus*

Gerard looked forward to Sundays. After church he'd walk down to the wharf and the coast where he made contact with captain Janson, the captain of the *Argus*. That ship was very different from the *Polux*, the sailing vessel where he had spent a year on Papa's crew. The *Argus* was a good-sized two-masted whaling ship, which was due to leave harbor in the early spring, when the weather got a little better up north. He and the captain seemed to get along very well.

Recognizing that Gerard did know a lot about sailing and the sea, the captain put Gerard through a grilling examination about navigation and sailor-ship. Gerard told him that his Papa was a sailor. He delighted in telling this captain about his year aboard the *Polux*. The captain's eyes lighted up and from that day forward, he took a special interest in this young sailor.

From that day on, all free time and every Sunday was spent at the wharf, learning about whaling. The captain understood how small and young Gerard was. He was frank and told Gerard of the hardships and dangers associated with whaling. This didn't deter Gerard. It just made him more and more anxious to get back to the sea, this time with the added excitement of a whaling adventure. But he wondered what Mama would say.

After church the following Sunday, Gerard changed his clothes and prepared to dash down to the docks.

"Hold it, Gerard," Mama threw out her arms and stopped him as he tried to push open the double front door. "Where do you think you are going? I need more wood for the stove. And I believe that you have some school work to complete."

Of course, Mama wanted to know where Gerard was spending so much time. He was supposed to be concentrating on his studies this year. With hesitation, Gerard confessed his new fascination with whaling and a hope that he would go on a whaling expedition in the spring. As Gerard had learned, there was big money in whaling, and the motto of the Koper family was 'work, work, and work'. So, he thought that maybe Mama would approve. She listened carefully as Gerard explained.

"The whalers get paid on shares. The bigger the haul, the bigger the pay they get. The *Argus* is a big, two-masted, full-rigged ship, home port Tromsoe, Norway. She has a skeleton crew and, along with the captain, they are all of Norse nationality. All conversation is in English, which I've been learning in school. It would be good for me and bring in more money for the family."

Mama took a little time to think this over, then said, "We'll see, Gerard. For now, just do your schoolwork and chores and we can see what happens in the spring." Gerard could sense that Mama was showing some interest.

It didn't take long for Gerard to find more excitement right there in Den Helder. It was a quiet Sunday in their little town when the church bells rang out and the town's men raced for the inlet and sprang into action. Winter was far from over in northern Holland. The heavy winds from the north sent high seas breaking over the dikes at the entrance of the inlet.

Between the coast of Holland and the island of Texel, there lay a big sandbar called the Haaks. A good many vessels were driven in there by northwestern storms and wind. If they struck the Haaks, it was good-bye ship and crew. Highly trained young volunteers went running to launch the lifeboats off the shore, ship their oars, and pull for the wrecked vessel. They had to shoot life lines to the wreck and haul the crew shoreward in the breeches buoy, one at a time.

*Breeches Buoy*

It was quite a job to save the crew and keep the lifeboats from being wrecked. It took tremendous strength and courage, especially in squally seas. This time they were successful.

A few weeks later, a big four-masted German sailing vessel got in trouble on the Haaks. A monster wave over the stern washed away their steering gear, leaving them helpless. All took refuge in the rigging in order not to be swept into the raging seas. Gerard joined the volunteers as they got two life lines aboard so the men could lower themselves out of the rigging and work their way into the lifeboats. In a span of four hours, a crew of thirty-six men was brought ashore. The cold and trembling sailors turned to watch in horror as the storm increased and broke up their huge ship, sending wreckage onto the Island of Vlieland.

As the volunteers shook hands and congratulated themselves for a job well done, Gerard found himself face to face with Captain Janson, his friend from the whaling vessel, who looked him straight in the eyes.

"Gerard, for a young boy you demonstrated more courage than a good many grown men. You would make a fine addition to my crew." Gerard beamed with pride. He knew that Mama would be impressed.

When news of the rescue of the *Catania* and Gerard's role in the operation reached Mama, she praised Gerard. Gerard knew that he was winning Mama over to his hopes for the whaling voyage.

Things settled down for the Koper family in Den Helder. Mama got word that Papa's crew had left Newcastle on her way to Valparaiso, South America, and that all was well. Gerard got back to regular routine work and school and keeping up the *Argus* contacts, waiting for the weather to break. He kept quiet about his hopes and plans for the spring.

In the meantime, Gerard passed this long, cold winter in true Hollander style. They were all great skaters. The canals were frozen solid and the ice was so thick that, in places, loaded coal wagons with four horses safely crossed the waterways. The larger waterways leading to Amsterdam and Rotterdam were kept open by ice breakers, so shipping was able to continue. But a canal running from Nieuwediep, via Alkmaar, to Amsterdam furnished the sport in North Holland for ice traveling. There were stands on the ice where, protected from the wind by canvas windbreakers, they sold hot coffee, fried apples, and bread. A big iron drum standing on bricks, with a roaring fire in it furnished the heat. The speed of the skaters was super-fast. No overcoats, just sweaters and a heavy paper jacket under them kept the wind from penetrating. At ten degrees below zero, the weather was about right for skating. They were even sweating. This was the winter bus ride in Holland. So, Gerard and his friends would speed off from Den Helder, past a lot of single skaters and horse-drawn sleds, past farm villages, and on to Alkmaar. After resting for about an hour, they made the return trip, good and tired.

# CHAPTER 4
# A Whale of an Adventure

Winter finally broke and Captain Janson told Gerard that he was getting ready for the whaling trip north. Now it was Gerard's job to convince Mama to let him go. He knew how to win Mama over. Money. Money was always scarce for the Koper family. Since he was a young child, Gerard had known that everyone in a Dutch family had to contribute. All children had to work in the family business, be it sailing or farming or furniture making. In spite of her initial anger at Gerard for stowing away on Papa's ship, she had been happy when Gerard handed over his small earnings for the voyage. This lure of more money did the trick for Gerard.

"Mama, I've stayed home all winter and done what I was told. I got good marks in school and earned some money at the furniture factory. I've proven my bravery by helping to rescue stranded sailors on the Haaks. But I am like Papa. I am a sailor. I belong at sea. Captain Janson has offered me a job on the *Argus*. Whaling sounds exciting and I would earn good money. It would not be as long as the sailings on the *Polux*. Also, it would not be as dangerous. We would not be going all around the world. We would remain in the North Seas. I have grown up a lot in the last two years and feel that I could handle the job."

"You may go, Gerard. I will miss you, but I do understand that this experience could benefit you, and our family." So, Mama consented.

With renewed spirit Gerard quit his job at the furniture shop, left school, and signed articles for a whaling trip north with the *Argus*. This time he was considered an independent adult, not just the son of the captain. He was on his own.

It took them about two weeks to over-haul sails and running gear, paint the ship, and get everything ship-shape. Tromsoe, located in the north of Norway was the home port of the *Argus*. From there they would operate in the Arctic Ocean. To pay for the trip north, they took on some cargo in Nieuwediep (Den Helder). The weather was getting warmer and they expected the harbor to be free of ice by the time they arrived in Tromsoe, in about four weeks.

They left Holland and settled their course due north until they came off Cristianson, passed this port, and changed course to north by east and steered for Tromsoe. They unloaded their Dutch cargo and got ready for the whaling trip. They had to build up their crew for the adventure that lay ahead. It was important to take the most experienced whalers they could find. The captain selected two harpooners and two extra sailors. Within a few months, they had overhauled their whale boats and gear, harpoons, and slicing knives. They loaded blubber-melting stoves and empty barrels in the hole.

They were not the only whalers in port getting ready to leave for fishing grounds. It was a bustling port with many people and boats. However, Gerard was the only foreigner among the Norse crew. They all seemed to like and accept Gerard, so they got along just fine. Languages came easily to Gerard and this was a great opportunity for him to learn both the Norse and English languages. He was certain that this crew would accept him as an equal, unlike the crew of the *Polux*.

When all was ready on the *Argus*, they set off on their way to the coast of Greenland. Excitement and anticipation grew among the crew as they all got to know each other and learned to work together.

As the third day dawned Gerard heard the lookout shout, "There she blows!" The whole crew burst forth. Gerard didn't know what to expect, but he was quickly drawn into action. He was filled with awe and anticipation for what lay ahead. Three whales were spouting. When a whale comes to the surface, he blows water through a hole high in the air like a fountain. This is a signal as to his location.

The more experienced crew members shouted orders, instructing Gerard as they worked. They lowered their two whaling boats from the *Argus* and rowed slowly to the whales, harpoons ready to throw into the whales.

As Gerard was told, "The big trick in whaling is to not disturb them when they are playing on the surface. This allows you to get closer to them for a good throw."

Then, at twenty yards the harpooners let go! Bullseye! Two harpooners scored a hit. The crew cheered. Then they were off!

The moment the harpoon struck, the whale leaped high, and then dove forward at a tremendous speed. In the bow of the whale boat there was a tuv, with about 1000 feet of rope.

Gerard was learning fast. When the whale dives he gets all the rope he wants. When he slows up, they pull the slack of the rope back in and make fast. Then the whale has to tow the boat until he tires out. After he repeats this a few times he slows up so they can pull the line back into the boat. They have to be careful not to get too close to that tail as he could slap it and smash the boat and crew to nothing. Repeated blows with long handled spears finish him off.

*Whaling*

After a few struggles they took the harpoon out and took the whale in tow. Wow, that was a wild ride, for both the whale and the crew! Gerard was both exhausted and thrilled. Then they had to find their ship, for the whale had towed them about eight or ten miles. It took long heavy pulls on the oars until they finally sighted the *Argus*, along with the other whaling boat towing another whale. Gerard would soon learn that their work had just begun.

They attached both whales to the stern of the *Argus* until the next day when, weather permitting, they could dismember the whales and turn them into whale oil and whale bone. They hoisted up the boats, cleaned up, and had a good meal and a few drinks. They hove the ship to under short sail and the watch below turned in. The weather was cold, which was in their favor now to keep the whales fresh.

The next morning, the dirty work began. They built a platform on both sides of their ship, squared the fore and mainsail yards, and installed blocks and tackles. This secured and kept the whales from turning around while the boys on the platforms went to work. They sliced the blubber off the carcasses and heaved it on deck, where it was cut it up and melted. There was a drain cock on the lower end of each drum and a pipe line attached to it. The whale oil was run into the barrels lined up in the hold.

Now in calm weather this operation was performed at sea. But in rough weather the whales were towed astern to a quiet inlet on shore and dismembered there. The whole crew was on the job and worked like blazes. Now a sharp outlook is kept for stray sharks, because they played with the whales and the men. After the blubber was stripped off the bodies, the whale bone was taken out of the head and the left-overs were cast adrift into the sea. It was a good day's work to strip two whales in one day, but they did complete it in late afternoon. And set sail again.

Early the next morning from the look-out came shouts of, "There she blows!"

They spotted a herd of whales playing on the surface. This time Gerard knew what to expect and burst into action. The same procedure was followed by both boats and two whales were quickly harpooned. Gerard's whale was a tough one and gave them their money's worth in a long fight. It was violent and the whale almost smashed their boat when his tail slammed down beside them.

After all that fighting, they ended up ten or twelve miles out and they lost sight of the *Argus*. After they finished off the whale and took him in tow it was getting dark. They sent up sky rockets, which were, fortunately, answered by the *Argus*. They had to pull hard on the oars toward the vessel. The other boat, which had better luck, was already ahead of them. They hoisted the boats and secured the whales in tow at the stern and called it a day.

As sometimes happens, the next morning, the sea was a little rough so they could not proceed with the dismembering at sea. So, they kept on course towards the coast, continuing to hunt more whales. In the next ten days they had eight whales in tow and made for the port of Reykjavik, off the coast of Iceland. They dropped anchor in port for about four weeks to complete the dismembering.

The *Argus* set sail for the Straits of Denmark, between Iceland and Greenland and made a good catch there. By that time, they were loaded to the gunwales and settled sail for Bergen, Norway, to discharge their cargo.

They had a good haul and made good money. Gerard was sure surprised at the amount of money handed to him. It was more than he got for a whole year's worth of work on the *Polux*. Mama would be happy.

Gerard had enjoyed his whaling experience. But he felt that it was time to go home. So, he separated from that crew and found passage on a three-masted schooner, loaded with a cargo of lumber headed for the north of Holland. After about three weeks he made it home to Den Helder.

# CHAPTER 5

# Lost at Sea

Gerard was so happy to get home and to hand Mama his share of the whaling money. But things were not so bright there. Mother had gotten word that the *Hildagonda* had been lost in a gale off Cape Horn. Papa and Gerard's brother were suddenly gone. Fortunately, Papa and his brother were insured. So, in one stroke they lost their bread and butter, Papa, and Gerard's older brother. Sadness overcame the Koper family. Fortunately, insurance money came through. Mama sold their property in Den Helder and they all moved to Amsterdam – Gerard, Mama, and Gerard's younger brother, Anton. That started a new chapter in Gerard's life.

The shipping industry had been changing rapidly, in Den Helder anyway. The North Sea Canal had been finished and there wasn't much commercial shipping left in the port of Nieuwediep. There was little money to be made there. So, it was time to leave that area. Mama was a good dressmaker and she opened up a shop in Amsterdam, allowing her to make a good living. In less than a month's time she had four women, plus herself, behind Singer sewing machines. It is hard to keep the Dutch spirit down.

A new and different sense of normalcy and calm settled over the Koper family in Amsterdam. Mama was busy with her sewing shop. Both boys were going to school every day. But that life was not in Gerard's spirit. He was a sailor at heart. After about one year, he got the wanderlust for salt water and ships. So, he searched for relatives who could help him. Three of Mama's sisters were also living in Amsterdam. One of their husbands was chief administrator aboard the Station Ship. The other's husband was drawing his second officer's pension retiring out of the navy. The third uncle had a café. A big family meeting was held and the adults all decided that the best place for Gerard was to join the navy. He was destined to be a sailor. Gerard was not consulted. But that suited him just fine.

His future was set. Of course, Mama was happy for Gerard to get to work.

Uncle Kasma, the one drawing his pension, took him over to the naval yard and signed him up.

28-9-81

The Marine Register recorded:

**Gerard Koper (age 16)**

**Length:** 1.43 meters
**Face:** oval
**Forehead:** round
**Eyes:** grey
**Hair and eyebrows:** blond

*Young Sailor*

Gerard signed articles for ten years' time to commence when he was sixteen years old. So, he would be committed to the navy until he was twenty-six years old. He would have to grow up fast. Training was to start immediately. Childhood was officially over for Gerard.

He was fitted out and shipped out to Leyden on the River Rhyne. There was a big training school there. A brig was built in the yard and boats for rowing exercises were made fast on the wharf. The men were housed in a big building and slept in hammocks. Everything was made to look as near to real ships' life as possible.

The commander of the training school soon came to the realization that Gerard had gone through a great deal of practical naval experience and so he was made number one in his class. He stayed there for six months, and was transferred to Rotterdam to one of the regular training ships, an old Dutch frigate. The classes had a hundred boys in each division and every six months they moved up one grade. One, two, three, four, etc.

In Rotterdam the men were dully hazed and installed. Gerard endured two years training and was promoted from 'boy' to 'light sailor' in the navy. He was transferred back to Nieuwediep (his old home base) aboard the *Van Galen*. That ship was ready for a trip to the East Indies around the Cape of Good Hope to finish training (navy style). Throughout the training periods the boys were coaxed along and graded for different occupations. This time they were fitted for 'navigation', 'boatswain', 'sailmaker', 'carpenter', and the rank and file. The lowest ones got plain 'sailor'.

After two weeks, they got shore leave to say good-bye at home. They then set sail on the *Van Galen* for the north leg of the trip. This being a final training trip, they stopped at quite a few ports.

This frigate (the *Van Galen*) was an old wooden ship and was being replaced by more modern steam ships. So, when they arrived in the East Indies, the ship would be sold for junk and broken up. These ships were good for training but too slow and clumsy for active duty and speed. So, the crew of 280 men and boys set sail for Cadiz in the south of Spain. All the while they went through drilling and maneuvers in good or bad weather, any way it came.

They were lucky to get a shore leave to experience bull fights, both exciting and cruel. The best experience occurred on Sundays after church when they gathered in the church yard to watch the fandango. This lively couple's dance was usually accompanied by guitars, castanets, and hand clapping. These events were usually followed by good wine. Gerard was now considered an adult, with no restrictions on alcohol consumption.

Then it was off again to set course for Dakar on the Atlantic coast of Africa, then head for Cape Town, South Africa. They settled in Simona Bay where they received quite a reception. There was a bunch of old Dutch settlers there who gave them quite a good time for about ten days singing Dutch songs and entertaining them. They put in fresh provisions and water on the *Van Galen*, rounded The Cape of Good Hope, and set their course east north east for Batavia, across the Indian Ocean, in Indonesia.

# CHAPTER 6
# Transfer to the *Melville of Carnbee*

In Indonesia the crew of the *Van Galen* was divided among several ships. Gerard was assigned to a sailing schooner, the *Melville of Carnbee*, as officer's apprentice in navigation.

About this time, more steamships were coming into service every day. Gerard's assignment was to chart the coast for navigation. They were to place buoys on danger spots by sounding depths of the water on the coastline. They also had the responsibility of locating just the right places for lighthouses on Sumatra, where the native population was hostile to the Dutch government. Gerard was familiar with Sumatra, from his previous sailings with the *Polux*.

A colonial army was stationed in Sumatra to keep order. The coast was blockaded by small naval vessels to keep the natives in line and to keep them from fishing on the coast.

About two miles inland was a line of block houses filled day and night by squads of soldiers. Their job was to protect the town of Oleh-leh and the two friendly campongs from the bad natives residing in the interior of the island. At six in the morning and six in the evening, the watches in the block houses were relieved of duty by fresh guards. At those times, like clockwork, the sniping rang out.

So, it was not safe to be around this part of the island. This hostility was new to Gerard, but he was learning fast.

They had to be on guard at all times for a surprise attack from the beach or from armed sampans off the sea side. With them it was win or die. There was no middle ground. Gerard's crewmates of the *Melville of Carnbee* were up against half savages. The blockading vessels were about ten miles apart from each other and two steam launches from each ship would patrol the space between the larger ships at night to prevent smuggling of arms and other contraband.

Daytime was not so bad, but nighttime was tough. Keep in mind that the *Melville of Carnbee* had to depend entirely on sail. When lying at anchor at night off the coast, they stretched steel wire and made some secure on the tent stanchions and boat divides. That protected them from any attackers boarding their ship from land or by sea. Rifles were stacked forward, mid ship, and aft within easy reach of every one of the ship's crew. In addition, members of the crew were armed with two revolvers each plus short swords for battle.

The weather there was steaming hot, so all slept on deck. During the day, they lowered their small boats and were out casting the deep sea and sounding the depth of the course to be followed by the coastline steamers. The steamers were getting ready to take the place of the native line of transport, including sampans, China junk, and vessels of all kinds.

The *Melville* had been laying at anchor for about two weeks, working on a difficult stretch of territory. The night was especially dark and dangerous. Then the cry of the forecastle look-out rang out, "Sampans!" In an instant they found themselves surrounded by eight or ten sampans loaded to the gunwales by armed Chinese.

Some had guns and the rest swords and knives. They were trying to board the *Melville*, but the steel nets prevented them from getting all the way up. Gerard's crew poured a heavy rifle fire into them. They sent up sky rockets and about four armored steam launches moved up to assist them. They were able to scatter and sink the sampans, natives, and all. Gerard lost two of his native crew. The steel nets had saved the rest.

The next day the crews of two patrol ships went on shore and punished the natives while Gerard's crew went ahead with their regular work surveying the coast. They did not get bothered for a while by the Chinese, who had learned their lesson.

Gerard was no longer just the optimistic young Dutch boy who went to sea with his father, the captain. He was on his own now, facing life or death situations.

From the coast, there was a road leading up to the main part of Oleh-leh where the post office, barracks, and white residents were located. The coastwise boat called at this port twice a month from Batavia to deliver freight and mail. Gerard's ship, the *Melville of Carnbee*, being on their station for over six months, dropped anchor there for fresh provisions, water, and the mail for their crew.

That day Gerard was ordered to go to the post office to get the mail. There was considerable native travel on that road along with fully armed natives who were hostile to the Dutch. About half way up the road a big native blocked Gerard's way and drew his sword. Gerard responded by drawing his gun. The native made no attempt to strike but in good English he told Gerard to sit down on the roadside for a chat.

He asked Gerard what ship he was from and Gerard answered honestly, "The *Melville of Carnbee*." He wondered where this conversation would lead.

The native spoke up, "Now, for instance. What would you Hollanders do if we came into your country? We offered a keg of gin first, then the preacher, followed by the soldiers to shoot civilization into your country? Answer me frankly."

Gerard didn't have to think very hard about that. "We'd run them out."

The native responded, "Now we got nothing against you personally, but the Dutch government comes in and enslaves a free people. They grab land and possessions, all under the guise of civilizing them."

He told Gerard that he was the leader of a tribe inland and his work, besides fighting, was propaganda.

The native went on to share, "I was educated in Rangoon, India. You are brave to travel this road alone, without an escort."

Gerard pointed out, "You also acted alone." They shook hands and went on their separate ways, each reflecting on their conversation.

*The Propogandist*

After getting the mail and returning to the *Melville*, Gerard reported his encounter with the propagandist to his commanding officer. The commander praised him saying, "If you had acted superior and high crown, you would now be a dead man. Gerard, diplomacy was the right course to follow."

Unfortunately, the mail brought Gerard the news that his mother had passed away. All that was left of the immediate Koper family now was Gerard and Anton. Anton would go live with his Aunt and Uncle Fiorani. Part of Gerard's salary would go directly to the Fioranis for Anton's upkeep and schooling. So, Anton was well taken care of. Gerard was truly on his own now. For the first time in his life, Gerard felt all alone, like an orphan, abandoned by his parents. He was sad and lonely and felt empty. The death of his mother was a significant passage in his life. In the navy there was no time set aside for grieving. In typical sailor fashion, for Gerard, work continued as usual.

While in port, the *Melville of Carnbee* loaded their fresh supplies, including six cattle and six hogs, plus chickens. They sailed back toward the spot where they had left off and went back to work. Every other week, they killed one of the cattle or hogs, providing plenty of fresh meat or pork. They got fresh fruit, bananas, coconuts, and mangoes from shore every day. They were living high, compared to Gerard's early days aboard the *Polux*.

Very close tabs were kept on all the personnel to know each one's ability and experience. There were different branches of duty to perform. First of all was naval training for general duty. It would take officers with special courage and proven ability to be a navy man. The *Melville* was for surveying. They performed hard work in open boats during the day, sounding bearings, and casting the lead for the depths and the kind of ocean bottoms, sand, gravel, or rock. Then they returned to the ship and marked the chart with the results of the day's work. Then they had to foolproof the ship for the night.

This presented its own challenges. The climate there was intense. In the inlet river entrances and bays, the mosquito crop was huge and plentiful. Between the mosquitoes and the natives, they were in hell. The climate was dry monsoon nine months of the year, changing to wet monsoon for three months. During the dry monsoon they roasted to death and during the wet monsoon, they faced storms, cool spells, and sheets of rain.

Sharks on the coast were plentiful and catching them provided a variation of routine as well as variety to their diet. But it was quite different catching alligators in a stream or river. They were sometimes able to catch a few at ebb tide.

They would take a bamboo shoot about four feet long, sharpened on both ends. They dipped the ends in oil then hardened them by exposing them to the fire. This made them as hard as steel. A live chicken was stuck on one end and a long rope was attached in the center.

One of the native crew stripped naked and attached a light plank under one knee to keep from sinking down into the mud. Half of the men ashore, armed with rifles, were on the lookout for a surprise attack by the natives and the rest got a hold on the alligator fishing line. The native with the pole and the chicken flapping his wings paddled toward the alligator. The alligator opened his big jaws for the chicken and the native thrusted the pole into his big mouth. The points of the pole penetrated his upper and lower jaw and the alligator was caught. That native who did the hooking would turn like hell and paddle over the soft mud towards dry land. The crew with the rope hauled him in. Oh boy, how that gator swished his tail!

He slapped it back and forth with such violence, trying to escape his captors. The belly of the alligator was soft. So, they had to turn him over and spear him or shoot him through the eyes. It was sure not easy to turn him over, so they often shot him. They let him lay there for a while then they packed their gear, called it a day, and rowed back to the ship.

*Alligator Hunt*

When they arrived back to the *Melville*, there was a small canoe tied up alongside. One of the stool pigeons, a friendly native, was aboard to warn them that they were planning a night attack. Now everything is fair in love and war, but they were warned. It may be a false alarm or a trap so the *Melville* crew got busy and set a trap for them. They were equipped with small sea mines, and were armed with four small quick firing guns. They strung the mines around the vessel at a safe distance. The guns were mounted, one forward, one aft, one on the starboard side, and one at the port side. All rifles were loaded and stacked on deck within easy reach. The steel boarding nets were unstrung, giving them a clear view, with nothing in the way. So, they were free to shoot, fast and accurately.

They signaled the other ships that were patrolling the coast, and asked them to pass the word along about a possible strike. The launches were advised not to get too near because of the mines. The *Macasser* said that they were well able to handle the situation. Now the natives picked on the *Melville* for easy prey because their only power was sail, but they forgot to think it was sail with teeth in it, ready to bite.

There was no turning in that night. After a good supper, and a few good drinks, the ship was made to look like everything as usual, as if they suspected nothing. They knew that the natives kept a steady watch on them. About 2 A.M. they noticed a fleet of sampans leaving the shore and heading for them. When the sampans came within about a quarter of a mile of their ship, things started to happen.

In the process of surrounding the ship to board her, they struck the mines and were blown to bits. The *Melville* opened up a murderous fire with rifles and machine guns and got most of them. Two of the men clambered on board over the bulwarks and they pretty near did have to kill them to capture them. After questioning the intruders, they found out that the natives set out to destroy the *Melville* because they did not want the coast opened up for steam navigation.

So, Gerard and his crew had turned the tables on the natives and put them out of commission. The captured were hung on the yard arm as a warning to the natives on shore. The crew swept up the unexploded mines and stowed them away for future use. But Gerard's crew was not done with them yet.

The *Cerum* and the *Macasser* ships hove in sight and along with part of the *Melville* crew, they organized a landing party. They traveled about ten miles inland and destroyed two of their campongs (villages). Every man in sight was shot. The natives were unbelievably brave. Men and women alike ran right into the fire and had a go at them with kleewangs or kvis. They did not quit. They fought to the last man. Some were armed with old style blunderbusses and a few rifles. A few of the *Melville* men were killed or wounded. All the wounded Chinese were shot and piled high and burned along with their campongs.

No Chinese were captured because they did not surrender. They fought to the death. The following morning the dead sailors were buried at sea.

The sailor's funeral was simple. The corpse, along with weights, was sewed into canvas. This was the coffin. The burying was up to the *Cerum*. The next morning, she steamed out to the shark infested water for about ten miles. The corpse was carried around the ship three times, covered with the national colors of red, white, and blue. Amid ship was a sliding platform. The body was laid on it and the captain read prayers for the dead. The emblem was removed and he said, "One, two, three, in God's name." The corpse was lowered into the sea. The funeral was complete.

The *Cerum* brought Gerard's crew back to the *Melville* and all went back to their assigned duties.

It took a long time to finish surveying their area. They had to complete the charting right for the exact placement for the lighthouse on the mouth of the river. Finally, they moved farther up the coast.

The telegraph system passed along the news that the *Melville* men were a tough crew. Although a few raids were launched against them, they were few and far between. Most gave up with failure and a loss of sampans and life.

# CHAPTER 7
## Pirates and Boars

The *Melville of Carnbee* crew finished surveying off the coast of Sumatra and got orders to proceed to Macassar Island off Celebes to survey the east coast of that island. It was a hotbed of pirates, who were notoriously cruel and bold.

The ship went through the Straits of Sundar into the Java Sea. They settled course east for Macassar and arrived there safely in four weeks and started their job of surveying the coast.

That was rough territory due to the Chinese and Malay pirates. It was impossible to tell them apart, the peaceful ship from the pirate ship. There were only three Coast Guard vessels to patrol this coast. There were inlets, bays, and all kinds of hiding places for pirates. The natives on shore were peaceful in front of their faces, but would stab them in the back when given the chance. The *Melville of Carnbee* had to be prepared at any moment for an encounter with a China junk.

Their first encounter came quickly. The junk was lying at anchor in a small inlet off the coast, busy dismantling a small native schooner. The crew of the schooner was sprawled on the deck, all murdered. Gerard and his crew dove right in. They killed the Chinese men who were trying to escape ashore. The natives came to the beach where the shooting was taking place. Gerard's crew turned over the schooner to them (the natives) and burned the Chinese junk.

The Melville called for fresh provisions of water and fruit. Wild hogs were plentiful on the island, which provided a good supply of meat. It did taste fishy as fish was their main food on the river banks. After getting all the food and water they wanted, they went on to survey the coast. Two days later one of the coast guard officers came over. He told them that he had gotten word that they were on the job, so he promised to call every two weeks on their trip around the island. After being told of their encounter with the China junk, the captain told them to kill anyone who approached them and ask questions later. He confirmed their findings that it is impossible to tell who was who out there. The officer left them and steamed to the inlet to investigate the burned junk.

The *Melville of Carnbee*, which flew the naval insignia, was safe from open attack during the day. But at night, lying at anchor off the coast, they were not safe. So, they were always prepared for battle.

While working off the northeast coast of Celebes one day, on an especially wild part of the coast, they noticed a small Chinese steamer, followed by five large Malay Sampans. They were steering toward the coast for an inlet off the island.

Gerard's crew lowered their boats, mounted their machine guns in the forwards and with half the crew armed, rowed toward the steamer. The rest of the crew stayed aboard the *Melville* for emergency, set sail, and followed them to help capture the steamer and engage and sink the Malay Sampans. Gerard's crew ordered the steamer to stop. When their order was ignored, they opened fire until she did stop. Then they boarded her.

Boarding an enemy ship is a risky job. They were met by men on the steamer trying to kill the boarders. It was impossible to know who was in charge, Malays or Chinamen. All they could do was to drive them all below deck.

The sampans were trying to escape, but Gerard's crew sunk them with gun fire and shot their crew as they were frantically swimming towards the shore. What the guns missed; the sharks took care of. Once aboard the steamer, Gerard's men captured the China crew and bound them, hands and feet and laid them midship. Their captain was a half caste, half English and half Chinese. The ship had been bound from Saigon to Macassar. They had been captured by the Malay pirates on the north point of Celebes while their engines were broken down.

Gerard's men ordered all up on deck. They freed the Chinese crew and shot the Malay pirates. Anyone who refused to come up on deck was shot. They placed one of the Chinese officers and a skeleton crew in charge to bring the steamer to the *Melville*. The Chinese were to be returned by the next coast guard vessels which came their way.

Once that was over, the crew all reunited on the *Melville*, hoisted up their boats, and went back to their regular job on the coast. It was not their regular job to hunt pirates, but if any case came their way, they had orders to eliminate them. The plan was that later on, the government would be able to place fast destroyer and coast guard vessels in these pirate waters. The *Melville* crew later received a special letter from the governor at Batavia for their two captures of pirates without a loss of their own. They were told to keep up the good work. It was surely a new life for Gerard.

The *Melville* was anchored off the north point of Celebes between some small islands, and every morning they noticed droves of wild boars swimming across the narrow channel to feed on the islands. Running short of fresh meat, they asked the captain to let a few of them go ashore to hunt boars to stock their larder. With a small boat, they rowed over to the island. They faced weeds, heavy undergrowth, snakes, and monkeys, which made navigating difficult. The boars were bold and armed with two heavy tusks used for rooting the ground or for defense. When attacked, they fought back viciously. The crew shot a few boars. But then the boars got tired of being shot at and charged. Three of the men managed to climb a coconut tree, while another man escaped to the boat. In order to climb the slippery tree, they had to leave their rifles on the ground and kick off their shoes. Then the boars started to uproot the trees. The boys in the boat moved up closer and scattered the boars so they did go back to the water and swam back to the mainland.

*Boars*

The gang aboard the ship was watching the proceedings through field glasses as the men returned with a load of wild boars onboard. That drew a huge laugh from the crew. It turns out that they were not afraid of pirates, but were tricked by wild boars.

The crew made plenty of hot water, scraped the boars, and cut them up. They salted them down, put them in barrels, and called it a day.

# CHAPTER 8
## Passage to Holland

After being onboard the *Melville of Carnbee* for four years, it was time for Gerard to be relieved and go back to Holland for home duty and a short rest for a month or so. When the coast guard steamer called the next time, he got orders to proceed with them to Macasser and set sail aboard the coastwise steamer *Surabaya* bound for Batavia. He must then report on board the station ship *Gedeh*, then board the Dutch mail steamer *MS Koningin Emma*. On his way to Holland, via the Suez Canal, Gerard was promoted to Third Officer.

Gerard boarded the MS *Koningin Emma* bound for Holland. This was her last day in Batavia, and Gerard was installed in a nice two-bunk cabin on the starboard side. He was to share his cabin with a returning sergeant of the Marine Corps. Gerard was classified as a second-class passenger on the large passenger list. There were officers, sailors, and soldiers from the Colonial Army, and civilian employees from the East Indian Government.

In addition, there was a traveling circus that had gone bankrupt in Singapore, and was now homeward bound for Naples, Italy, and an Italian zoo. For a deck load, they got four tigers, two elephants, a few jaguars, monkeys, and an assortment of beautiful birds. All animals were installed in good, strong cages.

*Jaguar*

*Monkeys*

The *Koningin Emma* left Batavia and set course for Colombo, an island off Ceylon, west by north. This was quite a change of routine and life for Gerard. After four years of hard work surveying, with his life often hanging by a thread, he now was on a luxurious liner with plenty of good eating, bathrooms, a nice comfortable berth, and even a barroom where he could buy drinks. Everything except the drinks was paid for by the government.

There was also a gymnasium on board for exercise and the circus crew entertained them a good deal. The monkeys and wild animals were great entertainment as well. It took only a few days for all to get acquainted and settle down for a pleasant voyage.

The weather in the Indian Ocean at that time of year was very changeable. Their only concern was the wild animals. If the cages should break loose, it would be disastrous. Four men were assigned to care for the animals and they did their best to keep a close watch. Everything went along smoothly. They sighted Ceylon, rounded the cape, and dropped anchor in the harbor off Colombo. They took on some cargo for Batavia and discharged some other cargo. They also put on fresh water, provisions and mail for Aden.

They left Colombo and set course west northwest for Bogotia, the entrance to the Gulf of Aiden in the Arabian Sea. They picked up the crew of an Arab fishing sloop that had been disabled in a gale and left helpless as they drifted towards the Indian Ocean.

Gerard felt that he was getting fat and lazy, doing nothing. To keep busy and learn more about steamships, he palled around with the officers and crew. He spent a good deal of time on the bridge with the officer on duty or with the boatswain and the crew on deck. He worked right along with them.

The first officer told Gerard, "You are the first naval officer I've known who was not too big-headed to roll up his sleeves and work along with the sailors on deck."

Gerard felt compelled to reveal his history. "I've been at sea since I was eleven years of age. My father and uncles were all sailors. I've been around the entire world. I've worked on whaling boats in Norway. I've fought off pirates and hostile natives, as well as wild boars. I've pretty much seen it all."

After hearing all that the officer asked Gerard, "How old are you, Gerard?"

"I'm twenty, sir," replied Gerard with pride. That was a real surprise to the captain. He couldn't believe that Gerard could have so much experience at such a young age.

Gerard made friends with officers and crew alike and learned a good deal about steamer navigation. That officer had also worked himself up from 'boy' on sailing ships, much like Gerard had done. That confirmed to Gerard that he was on the right path, professionally. The only difference for Gerard was that the officer was in civil service and Gerard was in Government Service. Big difference.

The captain continued, "The officers in the navy are mostly sons of the higher society class brought up from cadet, with a silver spoon in their mouth. They are a privileged class. As a rule, they are high-minded. Once in a while you find a few who work themselves up from the rank and file through hard work and ability. The ones who work themselves up from nothing are usually placed aboard vessels where rough and tumble service is required like surveying ships, coast patrol, and the few training vessels (sail) that are left over on the fleet. The silver-spoon officers are mostly placed on the larger battleships and cruisers. The tougher ones serve on torpedo boats. We have a few of these high-minded men returning on this same liner to Holland. A few have shown some high-strung behavior toward me and I don't mix much with them."

Gerard was certain that he knew who these men were, and he just stayed clear of them.

The weather was favorable and the animals behaved. The circus performers gave them some excitement by doing stunts.

The crew sighted Bogotia light, altered their course a few points to the west, and steered for the Straits of Babel Mandeb, between Africa and Asia. This is the entrance to the Red Sea. They landed the shipwrecked Arabs in Aden and proceeded towards Suez, on their way up the Red Sea toward the Suez Canal.

They passed the Twelve Apostles Islands, which is a series of twelve small islands in the Red Sea, called the sailor's cemetery. At that juncture, many ships, both steamers and sailing ships lay beached. The weather there was treacherous. Storms from the desert caused a short choppy sea and a heavy current. That provided an ideal spot for a wreck. The weather was favorable as they passed one ship. But two days later it was very different. A sand storm from the desert blew up across the Red Sea. Sand, wind, and high seas swamped them. They were between Mecca, on the Arabian coast and Yidda on the African coast.

The animal tenders and ship's crew got busy covering the animal cages with tarpaulins, and keeping the elephants and the rest of the zoo assignment from going berserk. Fortunately, the wind quickly quieted down. Everyone leapt into action with brooms and hoses to get rid of the tons of sand that had blown on board.

The animals were wild and restless. The animal tenders jumped right in to feed and settle them. A deck load of wild animals bears close watching.

A gale in any ocean or sea means lots of water, but in the Red Sea there is sand from the desert thrown in with it, free of charge. They were half way through the sea and the weather was clearing. They dropped anchor and awaited their turn to enter the Suez Canal.

In the canal it was two-way traffic, up and down. All steamers must wait their turn before entering. There must be no slip-ups or traffic jams. Half speed and following each other at a safe distance are the main rules. The canal was only wide enough for two big steamers to pass each other safely. At intervals, the canal was wider on both sides for steamers who developed engine trouble to pull out of line, while tugboats were made fast there for emergencies.

The people who took care of the canal lived in beautiful house boats, anchored on the banks of the canal. The native Arabs lived in tents on the canal banks. The climate was so hot in the desert that no white man could live there and be any good for any length of time. The house boats were all insulated so it was possible for the caretakers to live there. The canal was dug through the desert, which explains the heat. At intervals there were big dredges moored to the banks in the canal. Sandstorms, landslides, and accumulations of sand on the bottom of the canal had to be dredged out and dumped back on shore. Otherwise, it would not be deep enough for large sips to navigate. Those dredges stayed busy all the time.

As they glided past the canal banks, they saw caravans containing as many as twenty camels. These were known as 'the ships of the desert'. As they traveled from one Arabian village to another, they hauled goods, with loads hung on either side of their body. The driver rode up front, close to the neck. For passenger travel, they could go quite fast.

*Ships of the Desert*

Travel along the banks was extremely dangerous. The Arabs needed to be armed to the teeth because of desert pirates. Small troops of Arabian soldiers patrolled the banks to calm attacks of one tribe to another. Theft and murder were commonplace.

As the MS *Koningin Emma* passed ships from all nations, big and small, all the passengers kept busy rubbernecking (looking) at the sights. It was quite a thrill for big steamers to pass one another so close. At times, the passengers were almost close enough to shake hands across ships. In time, the *Koningin* made it through the canal and dropped anchor at Suez. They could let out a sigh of relief. However, now it was time for coaling and provisions.

The process of coaling was quite a sight. Lighters came alongside, loaded with coal and hundreds of natives. Eight gangways were pulled up towards the ship's decks from the coal barges, four on starboard, and four on port side. A man with a big bucket full of copper coins sat in the middle. The shovel men in the barges filled each basket and stood them on the platforms ready to be picked up by the carriers. That set up an endless chain of coal baskets coming up and emptying, then going down. Each time the fellow emptied his basket in the chute, he received his coin. The coins were strung on strings around their necks. Their uniform consisted only of a loin cloth and the string of coins.

The local boys found a profitable pastime. From the ship, men tossed coins into the water. As the coins sunk, diving boys went down after them. That was a new way for the boys to make a living.

The decks were swamped with peddlers and one could buy anything from a needle to an anchor. But theft was common. So, anything that was not screwed down or anchored might be stolen.

After the coaling process was complete and new provisions brought on board, the MS *Koningin Emma* steered out into the Mediterranean Sea, towards the Straits of Messina, between Italy and Sicily. The crew screwed on the hoses and got rid of the coal dust. Everything was covered, even the animals were black. That is why sailors don't like steamers. There was too much dirt and it was constant.

The weather was good and Gerard asked permission from the chief engineer to go down to the engine and boiler room to nose around and see what he could learn down there. There Gerard got to know the third engineer as they swapped stories. He showed Gerard around and asked Gerard to come down again when he was on duty. It was there that Gerard learned about the working of the engine room and smoke hold, all the while thinking that the knowledge may prove to be very useful. Therefore, for being a passenger, Gerard kept learning and making friends along the way.

# CHAPTER 9
# Naples and Gibraltar

They passed the Messina Strait without event. Good weather was on their side. After a few days, they sighted Mount Etna on the island of Sicily. They shaped their course due north. When close to the Naples shore they sighted Mount Vesuvius, a volcano, which was emitting smoke and lava. They dropped anchor in the Bay of Naples. The old saying is, "See Naples and die". That's because it is so beautiful, that you'd never find anything better. It is built with half-moon shapes throughout the hills with Mount Vesuvius in the background. Grape vine and fruit trees surround the bay.

Once they were docked, the passengers were notified that the ship stayed in port until the next day at noon. Anyone who wanted to go ashore was at liberty to do so. However, they had to be back on board before sailing or they'd be left behind.

The waterfront was tough and the streets were narrow. In the upper part of the town, the streets were wider and surrounded by nice residences. The city was well lighted and clean. After exploring the city, Gerard and his friend went back on board about midnight. The officer had to report for his four-hour watch and Gerard was ready for a good sleep.

The next morning the stevedores unloaded the wild deck load. Gerard was glad to see them go. A deck load is always bad. But a deck load of tigers and elephants is worse. Now that worry was over.

Promptly at 11:30 A.M. the pilot came aboard, sounded the siren three times, signally that the ship was leaving harbor. Then the head steward reported that one of the passengers was missing. Ten minutes before noon, the police harbor launch brought the missing man aboard. He paid his fine for disorderly conduct and the ship was on its way. Up anchor and set their course west, northwest for Marseilles, France, via the Straits of Bonifacio, located between the islands of Corsica and Sardinia.

Gerard took advantage of the period of good weather to spend time on the bridge with the officers on duty. Once in a while he took a turn at the wheel in the engine room with the engineer. He also took a pot of paint and a brush from the boatswain and helped the crew scrape off old paint and apply a fresh coat to the bull works. He kept busy and in good shape and enjoyed doing it.

The captain told Gerard, "For a naval officer, you are an exception. Officers don't usually work alongside the crew." Gerard told him of his past.

The captain fumbled and looked confused. "Captain Koper? I knew your father many years ago. You are a chip off the old block, Gerard. You would make a fine officer in steamship service."

Gerard choked up with pride and memories of Papa.

They got a spell of rough weather once but it did not develop into much. They steamed through the Straits of Bonifacio without incident and set course for Marseilles, France, west, north-west. They arrived there safely and unloaded some cargo and passengers. They only stayed there for three hours so there was no time for shore leave. They had to settle for just looking at the town from the harbor.

They steered south by west for Cartagena on the south east coast of Spain. They altered their course for Maragos, passed that, and steered for the Straits of Gibraltar. Gerard had heard of the difficulty of navigating the Straits. He knew that they were heavily armed on both sides. They could not see much of the forts off Gibraltar on the Spanish coast or Fangire on the African coast. Both were guarded by plenty of destroyers and battle ships. No ship would be able to go through the straits if the forts would not let them. They would be sunk by gunfire before they reached the straits.

The British control this sea route completely from the Atlantic through the Mediterranean to the east via the Suez Canal. All northern European countries use this route to the east. Australia, India, Japan, and China come from the east. If you shall not pass, you stay out. The United States and Britain controlled the main lanes of commerce all over the world.

The MS *Koningin Emma* steamed out of the Straits of Gibraltar, west by north. They rounded the cape and altered their course to north, half-east and steered for Cape Finnistere along the coast of Spain and towards the Bay of Biscay. The Bay is known for fierce storms and high waves and had earned the reputation of the 'Sailors Grave'. In crossing, a north-eastern gale struck them and the ship rolled too heavy for safety and they were compelled to hove-to. After about six hours the gale blew out and they resumed their course. If there was any coal dust left, the gale blew it off and the heavy sea washed it clean.

Little damage was done, but some windows on the saloon deck were broken. Everything quieted down and they sighted the lighthouse off Ushant on the French coast, the entrance to the British Channel. They changed their course east, and proceeded up the channel. They passed through the Straits of Dover into the North Sea and headed for Youden leading to Amsterdam.

As this was their last night out a sea, the captain set a nice banquet in the main saloon for a big feast. He congratulated the crew for cooperation during the trip and handed Gerard a nice recommendation for future use. The captain also told Gerard that he would report his good behavior to the officials of the steamship company, which could come in handy in later years.

# CHAPTER 10

# On Leave

The next day they picked up the pilot (someone who navigates the ship into harbor) who led them up to Amsterdam. Coming alongside the pier, two of Gerard's uncles, his brother, and some of his nephews welcomed him. They were all wrapped up, which was a strange sight. When Gerard asked about it, he got the bad news. It was the influenza epidemic, and people were dying by the scores. So, Gerard had jumped from the frying pan into the fire. He wasn't so sure that this would be a pleasant leave at home.

One of Gerard's uncles handed him a hip flask saying, "Drink this. It is the best prevention from getting the influenza." Gerard drank plenty. Aside from a bad headache, he stayed well.

Gerard reported his arrival aboard the Station Ship, drew some money, and got leave of duty for a month. He went home to Uncle and Aunt Kasama's house, where Anton was staying.

Anton was now fifteen years old, and it was time for him to choose a career, either to learn a trade or join the navy or merchant shipping branch of service. He chose merchant marine. There was a big old sailing ship in Amsterdam, where they trained merchant sailors and future officers.

Gerard enrolled Anton and paid his way for two years' training and upkeep. So that was Anton's new home. He got shore leave twice a week to see his relatives. But Anton liked the ship life best and did not spend much time with the relatives at all. Perhaps he was just glad to be on his own. Gerard took his savings from his four-year stay in the East Indies and deposited it in both of their names in a joint account. This raised Anton's spirits 100 percent. He was looking forward to his independence.

While on shore leave, Gerard divided his time among his three uncles and aunts. But he paid his way and spent a good deal of time with his brother on his training ship. Anton liked his work and liked the instructors, who were all old seamen, captains, and former mates. Some had known his father, so Anton was taken care of and did well.

One of the relatives, the Fiorinos, had an unmarried girl at home and they were trying to match Gerard up with her. Gerard did like her. But a sailor, who saw his wife about once every two or three years, was better off single. Gerard remembered well that his own papa, the captain, was always away at sea and was never home with the family back in Den Helder. So, Gerard wasn't interested in settling down just yet.

For Gerard, life aboard the Station Ship was too dull. A sailor served a watch duty once in a while, but most of the time he was left just hanging around, doing nothing. It was a very dull life but full of regiment.

8 A.M. Flag up. They stood at attention and saluted. Flag down 6 P.M., same thing. It was a regular routine of doing nothing except hang out and get lazy and wait for active placement. Saluting, listening to hot air, and drilling. Shore leaves every evening at 6 P.M. Back on duty at 7 A.M. So, it was all regular routine doing nothing but stand around and get lazy. Boring routine.

One fine morning Gerard was just roaming around the navy yard, visiting destroyers and different ships until he got near the dry docks. He noticed the *Astor* and another ship being fitted out, waiting for active placement and a trip. The ships were strongly built schooners used for observation and scientific explorations up north.

So, in typical fashion, Gerard got busy and started asking around. Being one of the last ones to arrive at the Station Ship, he knew that he had a long wait ahead to get an active berth, on either sail or steam. He wanted to be busy and get out of this dull life. He knew that in the navy you just do as you are told. You go where you are told to go. In the meantime, Gerard found out that the expedition north was a private affair sponsored by the government. That was why the schooners were being fitted out at the naval yard.

The captain of the *Koningin Nederland* was still in port. Gerard had made the trip with him homeward bound from Batavia. He had told Gerard to come and see him if he thought that he could help him. So, Gerard went to ask him if he could put in a good word for him to join the next expedition on the *Astor*. The captain suggested that Gerard get to work on the navy side first and then it may work out.

Gerard went right to work on his Uncle Verboon. He was the head of the administrative department on board the *Admiral Van Massirar* and close friends with the commander. That turned out to be a good move.

The commander told Gerard that he was crazy. He should just take it easy until he was placed in a more comfortable berth in the fleet. He told Gerard of the hardships that would be before him in the Arctic Ocean. Gerard told him that difficult was the thing he liked best. He liked being active. He always had. It worked. Two weeks later, Gerard was called in to the commander's cabin and told that sponsors of the expedition applied to him for two young officers to fill the job of third navigating officer aboard the *Astor* and another ship. They wanted men brought up onboard windjammers, used to hard work, with surveying ability who worked their way up from the rank and file. No featherbeds. For one, they asked for Gerard Koper. They knew of his training and he had come well recommended. The other men were to be selected by the commander. The rest of the crew was to be sailors who were on the North Pole expeditions before. All were handpicked and well trained for hard work and endurance.

Gerard's easy life came to an end. It was now filled with meetings, lectures, and working aboard the ship he was to sail on, the *Astor*. Gerard got to feeling like himself again, being busy and having something to look forward to, like seeing The Land of the Midnight Sun and North Cape. When he told Anton, his brother really wanted to go along. But Gerard knew that Anton would first have to train for a few years and gain experience. So, Gerard made arrangements for one third of his own salary to be paid to the bank once a month on their joint account so Anton was well cared for. In fact, Gerard believed that Anton would be better off that way.

After of month of preparations, the *Astor* was ready, spick and span for a year's stay in the north part of the world.

# CHAPTER 11
## Up North

Tug boats pulled the *Astor* out of the North Sea Canal, past Youden, and cut them loose in the North Sea. They did have a great send-off when they left Amsterdam. Bands were playing when they passed the piers of Youden. They set course for Stavanger on the Norwegian Coast, north half east. They got a good breeze from the port beam and set all their fore and aft sails and proceeded on course. A schooner, like the *Astor*, is built for close navigation and easy maneuvering but do not carry as much as a full-rigged ship. But they are speedy.

Summer was approaching and the weather was favorable. They experienced a few squalls once in a while, but none of the tough North Sea storms. The men got better acquainted and swapped yarns and shared each other's ability. They all became like one family. It was a very social crew. No high-minded stuff. All good plain men set out to do their job and do it right. That was a pleasure. Oh boy, what a difference there was between the misery days aboard the Station Ship and this crew! It was like night and day. Gerard was happy. For enjoyment and pastime, some of the men played instruments like harmonicas, mouth organs, flutes, and trumpets. They organized their own orchestra and had concerts at times.

They always did have a few fishing lines out, providing a good supply of fresh fish. There were lots of good educational books on board. Between their shipboard duties and all, no one was bored or lonesome.

Once in a while they passed close enough to another ship to communicate by Morse code and stay in touch with the rest of the world.

At last, they sighted the light of Stavanger and dropped anchor. They needed to stop for fresh provisions and water. It was a good-sized town, whose main occupations were lumber and fishing. The men were lucky to get shore leave in turns and enjoyed it very much. They stayed there for a week and then proceeded on their way toward North Cape.

Following the Norwegian Coast, they rounded the cape, passed Muvaanks and set course south east for the White Sea and Archangel (Russia) (Arkhangelsk). They passed a good many ice flows, large and small, drifting towards the cape. The men were excited to see some seals and even a few walruses on the ice. At that time of year, the ice sometimes would get loose and start drifting south. So, it took a sharp lookout to avoid collisions with ice flows.

They called at Archangel for some observations and fresh provisions. Their main industry was lumber, mostly white pine. It was a typical orthodox Russian town. The townspeople were uneducated and ignorant and were ruled by the Knout (whip party). Vodka was the Russian booze. Gerard thought it tasted like hell and he didn't like it. The weather was all right. Not too cold. There was daylight around the clock, day and night, at that time of year. It's called The Land of the Midnight Sun, for the sun never set. It never got dark.

All over Russia, the women did hard labor, the same as men. They loaded lumber ships, pulled carts, and worked in the mines.

While the scientists made their observations, Gerard and his crew were out in the bay, fishing in small boats. They caught plenty. They even caught a small whale that had gotten lost out of the Arctic Ocean and into the White Sea. The small boats were not equipped for whaling but the whale caught himself on one of their lines and, with their luck, the whale beached himself. The crew had only to finish him off. Gerard had had plenty of experience with whales.

Once in a while the crew went on shore for exercise but did not like it. They encountered a suspicious and ignorant bunch of people who suspected everyone of wrongdoing except themselves. That was the Russian style, making it unpleasant for foreigners. The scientists got what they were after. They up anchored and left the White Sea bound for Hammerfest, Norway, near North Cape. They were glad to be out of Russian territory.

They arrived at Hammerfest and made that their headquarters for observations. They measured the temperature of the Gulf Stream and made note of Arctic conditions. The waters of the Gulf Stream are warm, which make this part of the world fit to live in. The gulf runs along the North American Continent north to Newfoundland. There it disappears and reappears again on the surface around North Cape.

The crew completed their observations and bearings and left the harbor. They set sail for Reykjavik in the southern part of Iceland. This became their headquarters for observations in this part of the Arctic Ocean. Reykjavik is a small town with mixed populations-Icelanders, Norwegians, Swedes, and Eskimos. Their primary occupations were whaling, seal hunting, and lumbering.

The Eskimos lived in igloos. For heat in the winter, they burned whale oil and lumber. For clothing they used polar bear and seal skins and for shoes and boots they used bear skin. For the rest of the necessities, they depended on trading vessels making this port in the few summer months when the coast was clear of ice and navigation was possible. For transportation, most inhabitants of Iceland and Greenland had dog sleds and teams of husky Eskimo dogs to pull them.

During open weather, the scientists made observations of the sun, moon, and stars. They checked up on the current drift of ice and anything else worth noting. There was only one big drawback in northern navigation besides the cold. That was the closer you come to the North Pole the wilder your compass acts. The cold affects the magnets. In an effort to overcome this, a ship had two compasses. One was before the steersman in front of the wheel. Another was placed on top of a twelve-foot pole at midship to be clear of the effects of any metal fixings on the deck. Now about three or four times a day and at night they took observations of both compasses and with the help of a chronometer they were about able to figure out how much they were off course. Every measure varied a little but they could come close to knowing exactly where they were. Out at sea, a crew couldn't just trust luck. They tried to be as accurate as possible.

For a pastime, the crew visited the town and brought their band of accordions, mouth organs, trumpets, drums, and triangles along and gave the townsfolks a concert. They got a kick out of the little Eskimo kids dancing while the dogs howled. In return, the hosts set up a meal of polar bear and seal meat with whale blubber and some kind of home brew to drink. Gerard forgot the name of it. But it tasted fishy and made him dizzy. So, it had a kick to it. That was how the locals passed the north summer months. Swedish schooners made port and brought them tobacco, clothing, and fresh provisions for six winter months.

Each day it got colder and the ice started to get solid around the shore. They had to keep breaking the ice around the ship to keep it from getting crushed. They stretched heavy awning to keep the cold out and the heat in. Finally, they settled down for their winter observations and a little ice hunting once in a while.

Polar bear's main food was seals. Seals' main food was fish. So, their food was all combined into one. The scientists kept busy with their observations and Gerard's crew kept tabs on the compasses and some star bearings and kept a look out for polar bears and seals. They dressed Eskimo style with bear skins. To keep from getting lice, they greased the seams of the skins. But every night when they were below deck and in warm quarters, they had to pick the cooties out. Otherwise, the lice would get too thick and the men would be eaten alive. It was a nice pastime!

The natives started getting their dog teams and sleds in shape, ready to go out on the ice exploring for game. This turned out to be great fun. Gerard and his men had to wait until the ice got thick enough to go out hunting with them. Finally, six teams started out. They headed north in the straits off Denmark and located a big ice flow.

They sighted a few seals on the ice and the hunt was on. They drove towards the seals. Seeing the hunters, the seals made a beeline for their hole in the ice and disappeared into the sea. The men found their hole in the ice. They knew that the seals had to come up for air. The hunters just had to wait for a polar bear to appear. The men hid their teams behind an ice hammock a little distance away from the hole and waited. At last, two big bears and a little one found the hole and settled on their haunches around it waiting for seals to come up for air. The seals came up, the bears got three of them and the men shot both the bears and seals. So, the bears saved them the trouble of catching the seals. The bears were a great help. As the men were hidden, the bears didn't go after them. The men pulled towards shore and called it a day. It was a good haul, three bears and three seals all at once.

*Polar Bear*

Now when native Eskimos went hunting bears and had no fire arms, they had to spear them. That meant they had to get close, which was very dangerous and a good many men got killed that way. One bear hug and you would be done for.

Gerard and his crew pulled through a long, cold and dark winter. They were very glad when the weather finally broke. They finished their observations and set sail homeward bound. They steered south east for the Favor and Shetland Islands then altered course south by east and steered for Amsterdam.

They had spent one long year in the Arctic regions, cold and alone. Gerard was happy to report back to the Station Ship and take two weeks' shore leave.

# CHAPTER 12
## The *Silver Cross*

Gerard spent his two weeks' leave from the Station Ship visiting with relatives and his brother. He then reported back for duty to the commander of the Station Ship. When asked whether he wanted active duty or routine duty aboard the Station Ship to rest up, he immediately selected active duty. His assignment was on a berth aboard the *Silver Kruiss* (*Silver Cross*). He was to serve on the last old sailing ship in the navy.

They were to make the trip to Surabaya (in Indonesia), training a fresh crew, followed by dismantling the old ship. As we know, Gerard's history was with sailing. His whole family was steeped in sailing. His father and uncles were sailors. He had first stowed away on a large full-masted sailing ship, under the guidance of his father, Captain Koper. Gerard knew it would be an honor to serve on this historic mission. He was eager to serve. He knew that it would take the constitution of a horse to endure the wide range of climate he would experience, from the cold north to hot tropics. But Gerard was ready and eager.

Gerard's brother, Anton, was doing fine on his training ship and started to make small trips in the North Sea. He only had to serve one more year of training, and then he was ready for the big trips before promotion to 'able seaman'. Financially, Anton was well taken care of. He was happy and got big and strong.

Gerard left his relatives and his brother and called at the offices of the Stoomvaart Mastocappy Nederland to say good-bye to the gentleman who had helped him to secure the trip north. Gerard told him that he was outbound for Surabaya on board the *Silver Cross*, around the Cape of Good Hope. Then he got a big surprise.

All the big steamship lines in those days were controlled by the government and the coastwise navigation in the East Indies needed the help of naval men as it was growing fast.

Gerard had previously made a friend, the captain of the liner, the *Koningin Emma*, on which steamer he returned to Holland from the East Indies. He had recommended Gerard to the officials of the company and he (Gerard) had made a good impression on them on his trip north. They looked up his record aboard the *Melville of Carnbee* Surveying Ship and came to the conclusion that Gerard was the right man for a future job aboard the steamers. He was to be among a crew aboard the new steamers coming out for duty east. This would mean about six months aboard each new steamer, bigger pay, and a more independent life. Less red tape and 'yes sir' stuff. But first he would report to the *Silver Cross* and complete that assignment. Gerard felt that his career was well established.

So, Gerard proceeded to Nieuwediep, where the *Silver Cross* was laying at anchor, assembling the crew, taking on stores, and getting ready for the long trip east. The crew consisted of one hundred boys, fresh from the training ships and about fifty midshipmen for future officers, plus their regular crew of officers and men. It was up anchor, bands playing, set sail and they headed south west into the North Sea.

Windjammers were becoming scarce those days. It was a rare, beautiful sight to see one of the old-style frigates under full canvas, flying the Dutch Naval Ensign pass. So, most of the other ships steered closer in and dipped their flags in salute and signaled them, "Bon Voyage". Gerard and the whole crew felt a huge pride. The watches were set. Half greeners (new sailors), half seasoned men, and the boys took hold like a duck to water. All they needed was practical training and they would get that real quick.

With ease they passed through the North Sea and Straits of Dover, out of the British Channel, past Brest Lighthouse. They altered course south by west and steered towards Cape Finnistere on the Spanish coast. Then the wind picked up and the boys got their first taste of rough weather as they entered the Bay of Biscay. Seasickness hit the young cadets the hardest. The boys learned that the sea shows no favorites, rich or poor, all get the same dose of seasickness. Gerard and other seasoned sailors had a good laugh at them. In time, the seas calmed, their stomachs settled, and they headed toward Finnistere.

The calmer weather allowed an opportunity for training of the new young cadets. As they sailed along, they learned to speak to other ships by flag code. They passed one four-masted American schooner who had a heavy list to port and signaled for assistance. She held a cargo of peanuts from Dakar headed for Boston. In a storm her cargo had shifted. They needed heavy timbers and elbow grease to build a bulk-head at midship in the hold to divide the peanuts evenly and make them stay put.

Fortunately, the weather was fine and the seas were calm. The *Silver Cross* lowered two boats, loaded with timbers, shovels, and tools. Three carpenters plus about twenty-five youngsters went aboard. They set to work and after six hours the peanuts were level and safe from shifting. The American captain told the *Silver Cross* commander that he should send in a claim to New York to recover their costs. Their commander told him that it was just their duty to assist any ship in distress and to forget the cost. After much flag dipping and salutes both ships went back on their course. The schooner had been in luck to pass the *Silver Cross* because it was equipped to assist her. They had the manpower plus material to save them from capsizing in mid Atlantic waters with all hands on deck. Their windjammer carried a good load of special teakwood, along with picks and shovels and equipment to carry to the naval yard at Surabaya. This allowed the *Silver Cross* to save the schooner from being wrecked.

Upon arriving at Surabaya, the *Silver Cross* was given a special reception. The news of the rescue had gotten ahead of them by cable and steamer. New York and Dutch newspapers carried the headlines. "The four-masted schooner Three Brothers, owned by the North American Navigation Company of New York bound from Dakar to Boston, was saved from foundering in the mid-Atlantic by the old Dutch frigate, the *Silver Cross*. The *Silver Cross* on her last trip showed the world what men are able to do. Where there is a will, there is a way." The *Silver Cross* continued on to anchor in the bay off Great Canary for provisions and to give the crew a few days' exercise on solid land. As the name indicates the Canary Islands are the great producers and exporters of the birds all over the world.

The moment they dropped anchor they were swamped by bird peddlers. Gerard quickly found them there to be as crooked as in Chicago or New York. They sold two kinds of birds, singers and non-singers. Gerard noticed that the bird seemed to be singing beautifully. However, the peddler's mouth was shut tight, while it should have been open. Gerard knew that something was not right. So, he lighted a cigarette and pushed it in between the peddler's lips, forcing him to smoke. The minute he got the cigarette in the peddler's mouth the bird magically stopped singing. A little musical instrument in his mouth was singing, not the bird. So, his slick trick did not work. The surrounding crew had a great laugh.

As the *Silver Cross* sailed south, they neared the Equator and were stalled for about five days in the doldrums (no wind). They were among four windjammers in the same fix. They did have company when schools of flying fish and porpoises started playing around the ship. When a few leapt aboard the ship, the sailors got a few good meals, as well as a good laugh.

# CHAPTER 13

# Neptune

As the *Silver Cross* neared the Equator, it was time to get things in order for Neptune. Every sailor who first crosses the Equator must face initiation by Neptune. The young sailors had heard terrifying tales of what may lie ahead for them. They were rightfully scared. To calm their nerves, the older crew members told them how gentle Neptune would be. They told of the good perfume Neptune would use and the manicure they all would get, free of charge, plus a shave. The young men were suspicious.

They thought, "Maybe it wouldn't be so bad after all."

In preparation for Neptune, the mainsail was stretched between the fore and main mast and pumped full of salt water until it looked like a swimming pool.

"Maybe it would be fun," they thought. "This is nothing to be afraid of. It's only water."

The throne was built on the front end of the sail next to the barber chair. Then the young sailors spotted a tub full of special shaving soap. Unlike any other shaving soap they had ever seen, this consisted of chicken manure for soft soap, mixed with a little bit of scraping from the hog pen. A dash of perfume was mixed in. It didn't really look or smell too awful. The young wide-eyed sailors carefully watched the proceedings. They were suddenly not feeling very good. They were sent to their bunks for the night, left to ponder what lay ahead for them.

The next morning at daylight all were hailed 'ship ahoy'. Neptune asked if there were any persons on board who needed to be initiated to cross the line into his territory.

The captain proudly stated that 175 new sailors awaited his duty. That was a huge number to process in one crossing. Neptune was one of the oldstyle sailors, six feet two inches tall and dressed for the part. The officials clamored on board, took their places on the scaffolding built on the head of the sail, and got ready to perform. The sight of all these old, eager sailors renewed the fears of the young sailors. Then the ceremony began.

Neptune was handed a list with the names of the new sailors to be initiated. The young men were stripped to the waist so no shirts would interfere in the operations. Due to the huge gang to be initiated, Neptune needed to put two barbers to work. The barber helpers did the soaping and the barbers did the shaving. The shaving brushes consisted of two old four-inch paint brushes and the razors were two old filed-down saws. The sailor's eyes widened. They fell silent and watched.

Two at a time were called up and they obediently took their seats to be soaped. Each was asked his age. When he opened his mouth to speak, the paint brush was jammed into it. Then the barbers got busy. Back and forth over the young men's faces they went. In fact, the young men had very little facial hair to shave, so the barbers took it a little easy on them.

Once finished, the men were tumbled backward into the sail where a few of Neptune's helpers were waiting with stiff scrubbing brushes to give them a final cleaning. At the end of the sail there were a few crew members to give them a beating with barrel staves to dry them off. (They were really bathroom towels.) Two at a time, the men entered the procedure and came out the other side. Due to the huge number of new sailors, this lasted until sunset.

When all 175 were completed, the entire crew got an extra drink of gin. The boys were physically and mentally exhausted after the initiation. So they were allowed a day or two to rest up and pull themselves together. The new sailors could now look forward to the respect they would gain for having survived Neptune. In turn, they would probably brag about their bravery and pass stories along to new young sailors. That's how it would go, generation after generation of sailors.

The newly initiated gathered in small groups as they retired to their bunks below deck. Each shared his own experiences with meeting Neptune. Of course, they had all appeared on the verge of tears at times, but refused to give in to them.

Overhearing his crew talking, Gerard recalled his own initiation many years ago. He recalled seeing Papa standing on the sidelines, watching as his own son was thrown into the bath and scrubbed raw. Gerard's next thought was of his own pride at surviving the initiation. He remembered feeling his dad put a hand on his shoulder to share in the moment.

The memories of the year and experiences aboard the *Polux* flashed quickly before Gerard as he recalled the wild waters of the Horn, the noisy and exotic Saigon Harbor, the explosion of Krakatau, the fun in South Africa, rescuing a British sailing vessel, and experiencing the hero's welcome when they arrived back to the home port of Nieuwediep in Den Helder. That had been a big year in his young life.

His thoughts quickly jumped ahead to his year harpooning whales in the North Seas. Those were thrilling times, with money in his pocket and tales to tell his family and friends.

Then he recalled when his life had turned more serious. While serving off the coast of Sumatra, aboard the Melville of Carnbee, he received news of his mother's death. That left the two brothers, Gerard and Anton, alone. There was no time for grieving.

Gerard was now fully awake and proud to be serving on this historic sailing aboard the *Silver Cross*. It was back to work as usual.

# CHAPTER 14
# Johannes Drent

As the *Silver Cross* moved on, they received a signal from a Norwegian ship. It had run into rough weather off the Cape of Good Hope (south of Cape Town, South Africa) and lost some of her rigging. Two of her crew were badly hurt. As the sea was now calm, the *Silver Cross* was able to send a doctor over to investigate. As they saw the serious needs of the Norwegians, they added splints, medicine, and a few coils of manila rope. They also sent a spare job broom because, reportedly, theirs had been carried away in the gale. A case of gin and a live hog were also sent along to cure their stomachs and bolster their spirits.

To help with the repairs, the *Silver Cross* also sent two carpenters and a few able seamen. For support, the *Silver Cross* stayed by them for over eight hours until everything was ship-shape. After acknowledging their many thanks, the Norwegian ship continued on course. When they arrived in their home port, they reported the kind help that they had received from the Dutch.

The Norwegians had just been lucky. Oftentimes, when a ship encountered problems at sea, it was too difficult to get aid as the seas were too rough or the problems too involved for a quick fix. At that time, you would just be out of luck.

The *Silver Cross* made it to Cape Town at the southern tip of Africa and dropped anchor. The crew was granted shore leave and they did have a good time among the old Dutch settlers. Gerard applied for a week's shore leave to go to Bloemfontein to say hello to his father's cousin. The commander asked Gerard if he was acquainted there and Gerard told him that this was his third time around The Cape of Good Hope. He complimented Gerard on his experience and told him to keep up the good work. He wished Gerard a good time among the Dutch settlers.

Gerard thought about all the student sailors who had been working so hard to impress him. One stood out ahead of the rest. Gerard asked the commander for permission to take him along to show him the sights. When Gerard offered to pay his way, his request was granted.

They left by train for Bloemfontein. Gerard found that his relative was very old and his sons were taking care of the farm. Gerard told him about Papa and his older brother being lost at sea and his mother dying in Amsterdam. Gerard did brag a little that he (Gerard) was now a second lieutenant in the navy. He explained the presence of the young sailor with him. The sailor said that his name was Johannes Drent. After giving it some thought the old man said there were people by that name living about ten miles out. He offered to take them all out there the next day to meet them and see if they were by any chance related.

The next morning, they went out to the Drents' farm. After introductions were made, they all put their heads together and told this family history. They said that this man in South Africa was Drent's uncle. The uncle had been given up for dead for years by the family.

They told this story. When Drent's father and this uncle were young boys, they ran away from home and got aboard a sailing ship bound for there. The boys got on shore on a lark and got shanghaied on board a French windjammer bound for Saigon and China. They knocked around the China and Japanese coast for about six months and then the ship returned to France by way of Cape Town. As soon as possible, the uncle left the Frenchmen in Cape Town. An old settler took him out into the country and found him a good home with a Dutch family on a large farm. While there, he tried several times to get in touch with his family back in Holland, with no luck. So, he became a farmer. He stayed with his foster parents, grew into manhood, and married one of their daughters. He raised a big family on his own farm and was successful. And here he was today, right before their very eyes.

Drent cabled this news to Holland. The long-lost sheep had been found. He was back in the family fold again.

Drent stayed with his new found uncle for a few days and Gerard went back to Bloemfontein. They agreed to meet back on board when the leave expired.

After a good many farewells, they all returned to the ship for duty. The next day when the commander asked Gerard about his visit, he was happy to report about the reunion of the Drent family. The whole crew was then assembled on the afterdeck as the commander told the whole story. He also mentioned that through the boy's ambition and good will he was selected to go with Gerard on this little trip in the country and brought the lost family together after all those years. The commander mentioned that he would report this episode in the ship's log book.

Gerard and Drent went back to their duties on the *Silver Cross*. The happiest member of the crew was the boy Drent. He thanked Gerard over and over. Gerard told him to just keep doing the way he was. He had paved the road to success by himself. Gerard promised to do whatever he could for the young sailor.

They left Cape Town, rounded Good Hope, and steered for Cocos Island west north east, in the Indian Ocean. Three days out they picked up a stranded lifeboat. The twelve male passengers were half of the crew from the brig *Livingstone*, home port Cardiff, England. Their ship had gotten into a north western gale and lost both their masts. A bad leak had caused the ship to sink. The crew had left the ship in two lifeboats, but the storm separated them and the *Silver Cross* was only able to find one. The stranded men had lost hope until the *Silver Cross* came around. The *Silver Cross* cruised around for twelve hours looking for the other boat, with no success. They could only hope that the other lifeboat had gotten picked up by some other ship.

The poor seamen had been exposed to the weather for three days in an open boat with little to eat and drink. The crew of the *Silver Cross* got them all on board and within three days, they were brought back to normal. The commander asked them if they'd rather be taken to Cocos Island which is English or stay with them until they reached Surabaya. They decided on Cocos Island.

The *Silver Cross*, with the stranded sailors, proceeded across the Indian Ocean. When they spotted Cocos Island, they signaled the harbor and dropped anchor. A steam launch came out and took the *Silver Cross* commander to shore. He reported that they had picked up a lifeboat from the *Livingstone*, with half their crew. He told them that they had cruised around in search for the other lifeboat, with no success.

In return the Cocos Island commander reported a cablegram received from Singapore that indicated another lifeboat from the English ship, the *Livingstone*, had been picked up and that all were well. Hooray! All the seamen were saved.

Cocos Island was one of the British naval bases in the Indian Ocean. They controlled the four shipping lanes in the Indian Ocean. They had a fleet of warships in the harbor and were always ready for any emergency. Their commander allowed Gerard and his crew a little shore leave to exercise their legs and to say hello to the British sailors and take in the sights. The *Silver Cross* crew stayed there for two days and then proceeded on their last leg of the journey – to Surabaya.

The ship continued on course due east, rounded the southern end of Java and dropped anchor in the harbor off Surabaya, between Java and Madura. The final voyage of the *Silver Cross* was complete.

Gerard was proud to be among the crew of this historic old sailing vessel on its last voyage. But he couldn't help being a little nostalgic. Was this really the end of this graceful, large sailing vessel?

The company of the *Silver Cross* was distributed among the fleet in the archipelago. Johannes Drent got a berth on board the *Melville of Carnbee* surveying ship. Gerard got his transfer papers from Reserve Division to spend four years in the employ of The Royal Dutch Steamship Co. as second officer aboard the *Macasser*. He was to wait for the *Macasser* to arrive there from England.

The *Macasser* was taken to Suraya from the British shipyard by a skeleton crew. There she was accepted by The Royal Dutch Steamship Co. and the skeleton crew was shipped back to England. The *Macasser* (a coast steamer) was manned by a Dutch captain, first, second, and third officers and first, second, and third engineers. Gerard was the second officer. The boatswains, sailors, oilers, firemen, and steward were native Malay. That meant that there was a very international crew. Gerard understood that he would have to be prepared for anything that came his way. But he felt ready and prepared.

# CHAPTER 15
## New Guinea

The captain of the *Macasser* and first officer came from one of the company's steamers on the coast. Along with them came the second officer, Gerard, and the third officer, who was a greenhorn in the service. Fortunately, the new guy was a willing and husky worker. The engineers came from various steamers in the service. They spoke the Malay language and the different dialects used on the Islands. So, they were all set and waiting for their assignment of territory to cover.

The schedule of the coast steamers was figured to correspond with the big liners leaving the main ports for Europe, Africa, Asia, China, and Japan. They carried mail, freight, and passengers, and on average they made a different port every other day. They were kept busy at all times loading and discharging cargo and watching for dope peddlers on the coast, because when they start selling dope among the crew of natives, it's good-bye to order and discipline. The drugs made them go berserk like a wild elephant on a rampage. At that point the only cure was a well-aimed bullet.

The officers were always armed, both on and off duty. Safety first. The Malay was like all other Orientals at that time, treacherous. Now it was seven white men among a native crew of about forty so they had to be careful. And they were. The only way to make it all work was to be fair and strict. Treat them all alike and show no preference. Feed them well and don't be a crab and find too many faults.

The *Macasser* received their orders and territory laid out for them and left the harbor of Soerabay for Madura. They picked up cargo and a few native passengers. They stopped at Sumbala, Floris, and Timor loading and discharging. They also picked up about fifteen Chinese deck passengers. They were a motley looking gang and the captain warned that they bore watching.

The *Macasser* was bound for Papua, New Guinea. They steered east by north into the Arafura Sea. The crew was warned to keep a close watch on Chinese junks and it was a good thing they did. The next morning, they sighted four Chinese junks coming dangerously close and looking suspicious.

The *Macasser* could have out-steamed them but the captain wanted to force their hand and find out their game. The Chinese passengers got restless, so they were all herded into a bunch and some of the crew was assigned to keep them covered and in hand.

The *Macasser* was armed on the forecastle and on the poop deck with a machine gun. The crew manned them and the moment the junks started to lower small boats to come aboard, they were all attacked. The Chinese on board were shot or stabbed to death and the junks were rammed and sunk. The sharks did the cleaning up.

That part of the world was wild with bold pirates all over, ready to attack.

The pirates had planted a bunch of Chinese at Timor to take passage with the *Macasser* to Papua. Their job was to start fighting the crew while the pirates boarded the ship. But they got fooled. Gerard had been through this experience before, and knew what to do. They wiped out every one of the Chinamen.

When the *Macasser* arrived at Papua, they were told that a few months ago, a little English coastal steamer was boarded and the crew was murdered and the ship looted and sunk. The *Macasser* loaded a full cargo for Soerabay, including mail and a few passengers. All native passengers were searched for weapons or they would steal everything in sight, loose or fast. This was their standing rule. Safety first. Port officials were welcomed to help prevent the dope peddlers from taking hold.

As Gerard had learned, "When you get a decent crew, it's important to keep them so."

They left the Macula Islands and set course for the next port. When arriving there, they found the coast guard *Cerum* and the *Melville of Carnbee* lying in anchor in the harbor.

The ships had problems galore. They had lost half of their crew and a few of their officers to cholera. All the rest of the men were in bad shape. This called for quick action. The governor of the island cabled to Soerabay for medical aid and assistance to check the epidemic. The port was immediately put under quarantine. In a few days a couple of fast destroyers and a gunboat arrived with doctors and extra help. They got busy transferring the crews to Soerabay to the hospital up in the hills. That was the best chance of saving them.

The *Macasser* and the other ships were disinfected and manned by a skeleton crew. They all made for Soerabay to anchor off the coast until the quarantine was lifted and they got clearance papers from the port authority.

As it was the rainy season and East monsoon, cholera usually struck fast as lightning and, if under control, it would disappear fast. The best cure was a cool, dry atmosphere, and the best place for that was the hospital at Soerabay, built high in the mountains.

Up in the high mountains they had a European climate and, if a man got there in time, his life would be saved. The *Macasser* was tied up in the harbor for two weeks. In that time, they finished loading and steamed back to Soerabay to unload their cargo for the big liners.

The *Cerum* and the *Melville of Carnbee* were still under quarantine in the outer harbor and most of the men were in the hospital. The *Macasser* was taking on fresh cargo for Banjarmasin, South Borneo when Gerard got struck with cramps and a touch of cholera. He was rushed ashore and taken by ambulance up to the hospital in the hills. Before leaving the ship, the doctor handed Gerard a bottle of cognac and told him that if he drank it, he would live. If he didn't drink it, he would die.

Gerard was familiar with the healing power of alcohol. It had saved him before. He followed orders. The first drink Gerard swallowed wouldn't go down. The second one went down and so did the rest of the bottle. Gerard fell fast asleep.

Upon arriving at the hospital, the doctor pronounced Gerard drunk and ordered him to the observation ward. He also told Gerard that the booze got him over the worst of it, but that he was still in danger. Gerard was taken into the ward and stripped of all clothing. He was sponge bathed and left alone to sleep off his drink.

Upon awaking Gerard was hot and as limp as a rag doll. He was very weak. For relief Gerard poured a basin of water down his own back. One of the orderlies rushed up and told him to stop doing that, as a sudden change of temperature would kill him. As a suffering young man, Gerard told him that if he was to depart this life, he would, at least go comfortably. He was transferred to a dry cot, sponge bathed again, and made to swallow some medicine. He fell sound asleep.

Most of Gerard's belongings had been left on the ship. That is, all except a tin box that had about $100 cash. One day when Gerard was not feeling good, the orderly put his hand under Gerard's pillow to try to steal the tin.

Gerard grabbed the orderly's wrist and questioned him. "What is your hurry? What are you doing? You should wait until I've passed out. I promise you this. In case I get well you will get the best beating of your life."

The *Macasser* left port on her regular coast run and Gerard was ordered to spend three months on the Station Ship to recuperate and get his strength back.

The ship's doctor came up to Gerard and told him that the cognac had saved his life. Gerard told him the story about the Dutch gin in Rio de Janeiro keeping the yellow fever from the crew of the *Polux* and the booze keeping the influenza away from him in Amsterdam. Booze had saved Gerard's life several times.

"I owe you a big thank you, Doc."

The doctor kept Gerard supplied with alcohol the whole time he remained aboard the Station Ship.

In about a month's time, Gerard was granted shore leave. He told the commander the story about the orderly who tried to rob him and that he had promised the fellow a beating. He wanted to deliver it now. With a note to the head doctor, Gerard was granted the request.

Gerard took a carriage to the hospital. The doctor was surprised to see him until Gerard told him the whole story.

"Why don't you report the orderly and he would have been court-martialed and put behind bars."

"No, thanks," stated Gerard. "I promised him something and that would give me more satisfaction than a court-martial."

The orderlies were told to line up in the yard. Gerard had no trouble picking out his man. The orderly tried to back out with the excuse that he could not fight an officer.

Gerard slowly removed his coat and strolled calmly toward the coward. "Now we are even. There is only one difference between us. You are a skunk. And I am a gentleman." The line of orderlies broke into laughter.

The boys and doctors formed a ring around Gerard and the coward. The lead doctor blew a whistle and the scrap was on. They exchanged a few jabs and the orderly went down. He got up on the count of eight. When he made a pass at Gerard, Gerard grabbed both wrists, twisted them, and threw the orderly over his head. He was out, fast asleep.

The doctor explained to the bystanders what the orderly was trying to do to Gerard when he was laying helpless on a sick bed. He had just gotten what was coming to him. Also, he told the spectators that Gerard preferred giving him this punishment rather than reporting him. It was against rules but a great sport and they had all enjoyed it. That orderly was an outcast in the hospital and would be sent back to army duty.

*Fight*

# CHAPTER 16
# A Lost Career

After all the trauma of the cholera and the payback to the orderly, Gerard reported back to the Station Ship to resume his navy career. He eventually got better and regained his strength. He served on numerous ships, one ship after another, including new steamships and old sailing vessels. He traveled around the world many times. Like his father before him, Gerard learned many different languages and worked with people of many nations.

He had earned a good reputation. He knew when he had to be tough and fight for his life. He was not the gentle little eleven-year-old Dutch boy who stowed away on his father's sailing ship, the *Polux*.

His recorded navy career ended abruptly at age twenty-five while serving on the Hr MS Instruction Ship *Nautilus*, while it was anchored in Hellevoetsluis, Holland. The ship's logs recorded the following:

**"Day watch of Tuesday 15 August 1893**

---

At 2:30 P.M. Steward G. Koper brought ashore five crates with livelihood to deliver at the wharf. One of the crates was brought aboard at night at 6 P.M. by steam vessel and was taken from the hand wagon before the shop of van der Wiele. Steward G. Koper was temporarily arrested.

The lieutenant 2nd class at sea Delevant van Krimpen and H.S. Suermondt by commanding officer were appointed to the commission to investigate the content of the crate and to seal it.

## Day watch of Wednesday 16 August 1893

There was a session of the committee of investigation for the case of Gerard Koper.

## Morning watch of Thursday 17 August 1893

5:12 A.M. Reported missing steward Koper

## Day watch of Thursday 17 August 1893

East wind, fair weather, very warm

1:30 P.M. Afternoon parade. Steward Koper 21596 missing.

At 2 P.M. Lieutenant at Sea van Disk as officer of the day sent to Vice Admiral to report what happened concerning the flight of Steward G. Koper. Found that one of the life-jackets was missing. Sent Boatswain S. Steen and Hoeksman to wall to look for it along the beach but found nothing.

4 P.M. All hands before the bridge. Speech by commanding officer about what happened during the past night.

Temporary ship arrest of Sergeant of Marines F.T. Dievenbach because of complicity with flight of G. Koper.

8:30 P.M. Evening parade. Steward Koper declared missing

### Friday 18 August 1893

Brought back one lifejacket taken by runaway prisoner.

Missing Steward Gerard Koper.

### Day watch of Saturday 19 August 1893

Missing Steward Koper

### Day watch of Sunday 20 August 1893

Discharged as deserted on 19 August 1893, Steward Koper."

That was the official end of the naval career of Gerard Koper. He was twenty-five years of age.

His whereabouts over the next few years are unknown.

He entered the United States in 1898, although the port of entry is unknown.

Gerard was next reported in the 1900 United States census at age thirty-two. He listed his birthplace as Germany.

On the 1910 Cincinnati, Ohio, census at age forty-one his birthplace is listed as Holland.

In 1920 at age fifty-one he is listed in the Ohio census with his wife Caroline Oser, born in Germany in 1873. His two children, Elizabeth Koper and Viola M. Koper (my mother), were added.

Gerard became a naturalized citizen of the United States in 1942 and died the same year at age seventy-four.

*Wedding photo of Gerard Koper and Caroline Oser August 30, 1904*

# With Appreciation

The process of writing both books, *From Windmills to Waves, Gerard, Little Dutch Sailor* and *From Sail to Steam, Gerard, Back at Sea* was completed with the help and support of many people and events over a long period of time. My first thanks must go, posthumously, to my late grandfather, Gerard Koper (3/15/1868-6/19/1942), of Holland. He wrote detailed letters to my mother (Viola Koper Romer) with memories of his sailing career and his excitement of visiting many different oceans and ports around the world.

My older sister, Janice Caroline Romer Sherman (Jan) contributed her own memories of Gerard Koper and our extended family prior to my own birth in 1943. She told of her visits to Grandpa in Cincinnati, Ohio, as he and Grandma lived in an apartment above a store. Jan, along with our mother, compiled all of Grandpa's letters into a work they entitled "From Sail to Steam". These letters provided the basic outline of these books.

A great deal of Grandpa's official birth and family history was obtained with the help of Gerard Koper (not my grandfather) of Leyden on the Rhine, The Netherlands. At the Marinemuseum (navy museum) and Koninklijke Marine Nieuwe Haven (naval port) in Den Helder, I viewed numerous photos of ships and sailors of past years. It was truly exciting to stand at the very port where Grandpa sailed from as an eleven-year-old boy.

In more recent years, as I attempted to record and publish the true story of Grandpa's life until his death, I had the continued support of my family and friends. I gained a new respect for and admiration for my grandfather as he accomplished so much at a very young age.

I was fortunate enough to have such a wide range of friends and family members with talents in their chosen professions. Those who assisted me include David Hathaway, Michelle Hathaway, Christine Carter, Caitlin Hathaway, Kathryn Barrett, Farideh Sabeti Fathi, and Kolten Kubart.

In addition, my biggest thanks must be extended to Mary Caitlin Arroyo, the talented artist who helped to bring this story to life through illustrations. Her talents and enthusiasm were most welcome and encouraging to me to complete this project and bring it to publication

I appreciate the time and effort that you each spent reviewing my work and guiding me throughout the writing process.

Thank you.